THE SHUNAMMITE

A Faith That Pleases God

Willie Tracy Leggett

True Potential
REACH THE WORLD

The Shunammite

A Faith That Pleases God

Cover and Interior Page design by True Potential, Inc.

ISBN: (Paperback): 9781960024930

ISBN: (e-book): 9781960024947

LCCN:

True Potential, Inc.

PO Box 904, Travelers Rest, SC 29690

www.truepotentialmedia.com

Produced and Printed in the United States of America.

Cover illustration by: Christie O. Payne

CONTENTS

1: GREAT WOMAN/GREAT FAITH

*"And it fell on a day, that Elisha passed to Shunem, where was a **great woman**; and she constrained him to eat bread. And so it was, that as often as he passed by, he turned in thither to eat bread."* (2 Kings 4:8 KJV)

After reading this passage, I found myself wanting to know why God recognized the Shunammite as a great woman, so I set out to learn more about her. My first thought was: "What did God see in her that caught His attention in such a way that He spoke of her as 'great'?" In answering this question, I made it a point to study the verses in 2nd Kings, chapter 4. I wanted to learn everything I could about her life and then apply what I learned to my own life. I hope my findings will create the same passion within you.

I pray that my book will encourage you to search and study the Scriptures, which God has chosen to share with us, and then apply what you learn to your own lives. One of the most important things I find in these Scriptures is the woman's *great faith*—the kind of faith that pleases God.

FAITH

*"Now **faith** is the substance of things hoped for and the evidence of things not seen."* (Hebrews 11:1)

Where do we start? I believe we must first have a clear understanding and definition of the word "faith." The heroes of the Bible were men and women of great faith who believed God and His prophets. The Shunammite woman's actions convince me that when you have the *faith to believe* God, He will release the power needed to move mountains and to move in the trials of your own life.

> *For I say, through the grace given unto me, to every man that is among you, not to think of himself more highly than he ought to think; but to think soberly,* **according as God hath dealt to every man the measure of faith.** (Romans 12:3)

Therefore, I think the best place for us to start is with God's own definition of "faith" in (Hebrews 11:1) *"Now faith is the substance of things hoped for and the evidence of things not seen."*

When I read the Bible, I like doing word studies. This practice will also help you gain a better understanding of Scripture. Taking a closer look at the verse in Hebrews, you will find four key words: FAITH, SUBSTANCE, HOPE, AND EVIDENCE. Understanding these definitions will give you a better knowledge of faith and how to apply what you learn to your own life.

Dictionaries describe FAITH as "having complete confidence or trust in a person or thing."

Think of that special person in your life whom you have complete confidence in—the one who has shown distinguishing characteristics, especially on a personal, professional, or spiritual level. It could be your parent, a friend, a spouse, or maybe a spiritual leader or teacher—whoever has influenced your life in unforgettable and positive ways. You recognize them as such because more than once, they have proven to be reliable in their words, deeds, and actions, gaining your trust and confidence. At the end of this chapter, you will find a page for notes. Take time to note this person and what you admire most about him or her. By choosing this special person in your life, whom you consider great, and writing his or her name in your book, you will gain a better understanding of why God writes about the Shunammite woman and why He shares her story.

What do you place your confidence in? For you hunters, your confidence is in your favorite rifle, and for you fishermen, it is in your rod and reel combo. When I play golf, my go-to club is my Mizuno Wings pitching wedge, in which I have total confidence. When I am 100 yards from the green, I reach for it, knowing I can hit it 100 yards 90% of the time. Most likely, I will make birdie or par that hole. Confidence is a game changer!

I know the Shunammite woman never saw a golf club or attended the US Open, but this one thing I do know: she lived her life to the fullest. In doing so, she knew how valuable it was to have confident "faith" in people and things, especially when it came to God and His prophet.

I find these passages filled with tremendous amounts of knowledge, wisdom, and faith, evidenced by her deep passion to serve God and His servant Elisha. I believe her willingness to supply whatever the

> This one thing I do know: she lived her life to the fullest.

man of God needed is one reason God introduced her to His church, the Body of Christ, as a *great* woman. I also know that the things you learn about her life will help your own personal walk with God and strengthen your faith, as it has my own.

THE FAITH OF A GREAT WOMAN

Throughout Scripture, God uses many people like the Shunammite woman—I call them "Heroes of Faith"—to encourage us spiritually and to build our own faith. Hebrews 11 is known as the faith chapter. In verse 4, we find: "By faith Abel offered unto God a more excellent sacrifice." Verse 7 states, "By faith Noah, being warned of God of things not seen yet, moved with fear, prepared an ark to the saving of his house [family]." Verse 31 states: "By faith, the harlot Rahab perished not with them that believed not, when she had received the spies with peace." Please take the time to read Hebrews 11 in its entirety.

The Shunammite woman spent a lot of quality time with Elisha, and her faith grew stronger as they fellowshipped together. I pray you will be inspired and challenged by her life. Try to imagine yourself with her during her happy times, the sad times, and those times when her trials brought her much despair. Through it all, her faith in God made her more than an overcomer, bringing her great joy.

"And she said unto her husband, behold now, I perceive that this is a holy man of God, which passeth by us continually." (2 Kings 4:9)

The Shunammite woman's example is extremely clear: if your desire is to have great faith, you must surround yourself with men and women of great faith. She not only noticed Elisha by his many visits, but she also spent time with him on a personal and spiritual level. I believe that hearing his testimonies of the many miracles God performed at his hands, she was convinced that he truly was a holy man of God.

Likewise, expect your faith to increase only if you are spending time with people who will encourage you through your deepest valley, when things are not going well. During these times, you need people who know how important it is to speak words of life over you, not words of doubt and unbelief.

The righteous choose their friends carefully (Proverbs 12:26 NIV).

In 1992, I served as lead pastor of Munson Assembly of God Church in Munson, Florida. One day, I received a phone call from a family in our community, asking if I would meet them at Sacred Heart Hospital in Pensacola, Florida, to pray for their mother. After our conversation, I called two elders of the church, inviting them to go with me. When we arrived at the hospital, we went to the progressive care unit on the fourth floor.

After speaking with the family, I read (James 5:14-15):

> *Is any sick among you? Let him call for the elders of the church; and let them pray over him, anointing him with oil in the name of the Lord: And the prayer of FAITH shall save the sick, and the Lord shall raise him up; and if he has committed sins, they shall be forgiven him.*

Being a young, born-again believer, I was convinced that anything I asked in faith and believing, God would do. Can I get a witness? After anointing her with oil, I prayed for the Lord to heal her and for His healing power to touch her. She made a full recovery and was released a few days later. Praise God!

As we were leaving the progressive care unit, one of the elders made a remark that I will never forget, saying: "She really looks bad, I don't think she's going to make it." While he was speaking, God spoke to me: "Be careful whom you ask to go with you, when you need to pray the prayer of faith." At that moment, I realized that it is better to go alone than to have someone with a doubting spirit or one who is not in agreement.

*"Again, I say unto you, **that if two of you shall agree on earth as touching anything that they shall ask, it shall be done for them** of my Father which is in heaven."* (Matthew 18:19)

As people of faith, we understand the importance of fellowship and breaking bread together. In verse 8 of 2 Kings, Chapter 4, we see the Shunammite woman supplying bread for Elisha. The more time she spent with the man of God, the more she desired to worship God.

"Let us make a little chamber, I pray thee, on the wall; and let us set for him there a bed, and a table, and a stool, and a candlestick: and it shall be, when he cometh to us, that he shall turn in thither." (2 Kings 4:10)

Here we find the Shunammite woman wanted more than a casual visit. More than just breaking bread together, she was ready to have a personal relationship. She was seeking a spiritual relationship, and she was ready and willing to invest her time and resources to create a place of worship. She therefore asked her husband's permission to build a little chamber on the side of the house.

Notice the care she took in designing his room. Her desire was to make his room inviting by placing a bed there to ensure he had a comfortable place to rest during the day, and if needed, he could spend the night. She also added a table and stool to create a place to study or eat his meals. Finally, the room was not complete without the candlestick to give light for the man of God as he rested from the elements. In those days, he likely walked on hot and dusty roads for hours.

I believe that during the time Elisha left to minister in nearby towns, she would prepare the room for his return: sweeping the floor, putting clean sheets on the bed, removing the dirty water from the basin, replacing the old bread with fresh bread, adding clean water for drinking, then removing the old wax and replacing it with a new candlestick. Light is especially important to our Christian faith.

We are the temples of the Holy Spirit. God's desire is to reside in you, not in rooms or temples made of wood and stone.

As I write this chapter, it is as though I am there watching her as she goes about her tasks. She has no idea—the importance of having Elisha's room and bed clean, prepared, and ready to receive him and how these acts of love will play a major role for God to perform an unforeseen miracle. This reminds me: the Bible says we are the temples of the Holy Spirit. God's desire is to reside in you, not in rooms or temples made of wood and stone.

Therefore, start today preparing for tomorrow's unforeseen miracles. Let us use Elisha's room and the items placed therein as our spiritual blueprint to prepare our temples and create within ourselves a place that will be pleasing and inviting for the Holy Spirit to come and dwell.

Spiritually, there is much to learn from this room. You may think that it was only a little chamber, but to the Shunammite woman, it was a great sacrifice. She was all in—totally committed to God! Keeping his room clean was another way of letting Elisha know that he would always be welcome in her home. She reminds us that we are temples, and therefore, we should always be clean and ready to receive God's Spirit.

Her experience with Elisha is very much like our own salvation experience. First, she heard about Elisha, as we have heard about Jesus. She spent time with Elisha, as we spend time with Jesus by attending church. She came to realize he was a holy man of God, as we come to realize that Jesus is the Savior of the world. She built him a little chamber to abide in, and we invite Jesus to come into our hearts and abide in us—the temples of His Holy Spirit.

"In whom ye also trusted, after that ye heard the word of truth, the gospel of your salvation: in whom also after that ye believed, ye were sealed with that Holy Spirit of promise." (Ephesians 1:13)

Another thing we learn from the Shunammite woman is that she does not offer Elisha her old, rundown shed in the backyard. She built **a new and clean room.** When you prepare your temple to receive God's Holy Spirit, do not give Him yesterday's worship, yesterday's praise, or yesterday's shout. Sing Him a new song, shout Him a new praise, and give to Him your new worship with a new and clean heart. She gave the prophet her best, and God requires from us our best. As you prepare to receive the Holy Spirit, give God the best you have. Think of the cost.

Her dedication to please God has challenged me, especially how I approach God and the trials in my personal life. Now when given a task—no matter the size—I remember the little chamber she built in her home and the love and care she showed when building and furnishing it for the man of God. Her passion has totally changed how I think when it comes to the smallest of tasks. We must apply ourselves 100% to every task.

The Bible tells us that whatever we do in word or deed, we must do it as unto the Lord. The Shunammite woman truly exemplifies that Scripture to its fullness. *"And whatsoever ye do in word or deed, do all in the name of the lord Jesus, giving thanks to God and the Father by him."* (Colossians 3:17)

"And the king said unto Araunah, 'Nay; but I will surely buy it from thee at a price; **neither will I offer burnt offerings unto the Lord my God of that which doth cost me nothing.'"** (2 Samuel 24:24)

Here is a good place to start: *"Therefore if any man be in Christ, he is a new creature: old things are passed away; behold, all things are become **new.** "* (2 Corinthians 5:17) God is searching the hearts of men and women, looking for new vessels with clean "hearts" to be temples of his Holy Spirit.

*"Create in me a **clean** heart, O God; and renew a right spirit within me."* (Psalms 51:10)

PURE MOTIVES

The Shunammite woman had a pure heart with pure motives. Always check your motives; your motives always should be to give glory and honor to your heavenly Father.

The Holy Spirit is urging me to write this insert, knowing the enemy of your soul will cause you to struggle with past disappointments and sins. Satan will attempt to convince you that you will never be good enough, clean enough, or new enough to be accepted by God. If you allow it, he will keep you trapped in your past, but your past does not define who you are. God has given you the freedom to receive His miracle of new beginnings. *"For [Satan] is a liar, and the father of it."* (John 8:44)

Let's break his stronghold. Pray this simple but powerful prayer: "Jesus, I surrender all my past disappointments and sins to you and ask you to please forgive me and create in me a new and clean heart. Amen."

> *Brethren, I count not myself to have apprehended: but this one thing I do, forgetting those things which are behind, and reaching forth unto those things which are before, I press toward the mark for the prize of the high calling of God in Christ Jesus.*
> (Philippians 3:13-14)

Now that you have prayed, God has heard and cast away your sins. *"As far as the east is from the west, so far has he removed your transgressions from you."* (Psalms 103:12) Yes, that's right! Did I hear you shout, "THANK YOU JESUS"? I believe I did. Brothers and sisters, you are forgiven. Now take the energy you once used, worrying over things that you could not change, to positive energy of thanksgiving, worship, and praise, for He inhabits your praise. **He loves it**. *"But thou art holy, O thou that inhabits the praises of Israel."* (Psalms 22:3)

You have created an environment that is refreshing, relaxing, and a place where you can minister to the Holy Spirit and your Savior Jesus Christ.

The most important item the Shunammite woman placed in the room was the candlestick. Light brings comfort, peace, security, and power. Take a moment to remember that unforgettable thunderstorm in your own life. The winds were frightening, blowing rain and hail against the windows. Suddenly, a blinding flash of lightning shot across the sky, followed by thunder that shook the house, knocking out the power and the lights. Your conversation probably sounded something like this:

"Honey, where is the flashlight?"

"I don't know. You had it last."

"Well, I cannot find it anywhere."

"You never put things back in their place! Ouch!"

"What happened?"

"I stubbed my toe on the coffee table. I give up. Where are the candles?"

Sound familiar? During all the chaos and while you were trying to make your way down the pitch-black hallway, the power is restored and with the power, the lights, and with the lights, once again your comfort, peace, and security. Of course, apologies to one another come swiftly. Been there, done that!

So it is with you. Without God's light, you are living a life of chaos. As soon as His marvelous light enters you, His forgiveness, comfort, peace, security, power, and a measure of faith come as well, bringing you great joy.

Learning from the Shunammite woman's example. She put her faith in God and His prophet, so your Christian walk will totally depend on your faith in Jesus Christ who lights your path.

You are most likely thinking, "How can I light my temple?" *"When Jesus spoke again to the people, he said,* **'I am the light of the world. Whoever follows me will never walk in darkness but will have the light of life.'"** (John 8:12) The moment you repent and ask Jesus to forgive you of your sins, confessing him as your Lord and Savior, His wonderful light enters you, and you instantly receive a measure of faith which He promises to all believers. Maintain your temple!

Never give up on your dreams, and never give up on God!

Miracles manifest when you totally surrender yourself to God. At that moment, you will begin to see His miracles. I am writing this book to take you beyond your fears and doubt to the promises of God which He will perform in your life.

HER FAITH IS CHALLENGED.

Soon, the Shunammite woman received for her labor of love, a long-awaited miracle, but the words of the Prophet Elisha tested her faith. Throughout the Bible, we find when God's people obey, honor, and respect Him, His blessings soon follow.

Are you ready to receive your miracle and blessings? If so, get ready to have your faith challenged, beginning with a word from God—not the written word alone, but His spoken word. Yes, you read it right, His spoken word. Your first miracle most likely will be hearing God speak to you in His small, still voice, and then having the faith to believe and do what He asks of you. In the Old Testament, God spoke to his prophets. In turn, they spoke to the people. Today, not only does He speak through His prophets and preachers, but He also speaks directly to you: *"My sheep hear my voice, and I know them, and they follow me."* (John 10:27)

Although many in the Body of Christ have not heard God speak, I believe there is an easy explanation for this. God speaks to those who have the faith and desire to hear Him—those who know His voice and believe His word. Maybe you have heard His voice, but out of fear, you did not do what He asked you to do. **LET'S be real.** When God speaks, His words can and most likely will take you out of your comfort zone.

> *And the LORD called Samuel again the third time. And he arose and went to Eli, and said, "Here am I, for thou didst call me." And Eli perceived that the LORD had called the child. Therefore, Eli said unto Samuel, "Go, lie down; and it shall be, if he calls thee, that thou shalt say, Speak, LORD, for thy servant heareth." So Samuel went and lay down in his place. And the LORD came, and stood, and called as at other times, "Samuel, Samuel.' Then Samuel answered, 'Speak, for thy servant heareth."* (1 Samuel 3:8-10)

This was Samuel's first time hearing God speak. Like Samuel, we all experience our first time, hearing His voice. **Don't disappoint Him.**

WITHOUT FAITH IT IS IMPOSSIBLE TO PLEASE GOD.

"And he said, about this season, according to the time of life, thou shalt embrace a son. And she said, Nay, my lord, thou man of God, do not lie unto thine handmaid." (2 Kings 4:16)

When the Shunammite woman heard from Elisha that she would have a child, her first reaction was to doubt. Her faith and belief in Elisha instantly changed from his being a holy man of God, to a man she could no longer trust, believing him to be a liar.

Hearing his words challenged her faith. Now she thought, "Who could perform such a miracle, the miracle of life?" Could it be that his words reminded her of the many restless and sleepless nights she wept while praying for a child, only to receive unanswered prayers? It could be that she resolved she would never have children, and she was okay with that. However, hearing the prophet's words brought back all the painful memories. Soon, she would find that with the God she served, loved, and worshiped—in Him, all things were possible.

> Soon, she would find that with the God she served, loved, and worshiped—in Him, all things were possible.

"And Jesus looking upon them saith, with men it is impossible, but not with God: for with God all things are possible." (Mark 10:27) Thinking in her flesh, she realized that it was impossible for her and her husband to have a child because of his age. Again, she was thinking of all the negatives in conceiving and bearing a child, but it was not about their ability and strength. It was about God's promise.

So it is with you when God tells you that He is going to perform a miracle in your life or use you as the vessel to work miracles in another person's life. If you are not careful, your mind will cause you to think as people without hope, believing that miracles will never happen for you. How many times have you said that very same thing?

With God, all things are possible. I can only imagine how she must have felt when her child kicked and moved for the first time. I know there was some shouting going on in the Shunammite home. Hallelujah! I believe she jumped with joy, knowing God's promise had come to fruition, that she would truly have the promised child she so desperately wanted.

HER FAITH IS RESTORED IN ELISHA.

Think about this fact: after many years of praying, her prayers were finally answered when she built the little room for the man of God. Out of that very room, God answered her prayers. You need to invite God into your space; you need a close and personal relationship with Him. In this place, you will be able to hear His voice.

What about your miracle—the one you have been waiting for, but as the days, weeks, months, and years have passed, the waiting has caused you to doubt God and His promises? Have you given up and begun speaking words of doubt that it will never happen? Could it be that you have stopped believing, praying, or trusting in God? Have you given up on your dreams?

Never give up on your dreams, and never give up on God!

Miracles manifest when you have the faith to totally surrender yourself to God as the Shunammite woman did. At that very moment, you will begin to see His miracles. I am writing this book to take you beyond your fear and unbelief to the promises of God which He will perform in your life.

"Faith untried may be true faith, but it is sure to be little faith, and it is likely to remain dwarfish so long as it is without trials" —C.H. Spurgeon

GOD KEEPS HIS PROMISES—SO YOU KEEP THE FAITH.

NOTES:

_____
_____
_____
_____
_____
_____
_____
_____
_____
_____
_____
_____
_____
_____
_____
_____
_____
_____
_____
_____
_____
_____
_____
_____
_____
_____
_____
_____

2: SUBSTANCE

*"Now faith is the **substance** of things hoped for and the evidence of things not seen."* (Hebrews 11:1)

"Substance": The subject matter of thought.

THE SEASON OF LIFE

On this day, the Prophet Elisha and his servant Gehazi turned into the chamber to rest from their journey, and while resting, they discussed what could be done for the Shunammite woman. Elisha then sent his servant to ask her, "You have been so kind to me with all this care. What can I do for you?" So, the servant asked her, "What would you have Elisha do for you? Speak to the king on your behalf or the captain of the host?" She answered that this was not necessary, for she lived among her own people. Gehazi returned with her answer. Again, Elisha said, "There must be something she needs."

"And he said, what then is to be done for her? And Gehazi answered, verily she hath no child, and her husband is old." (2 Kings 4:14)

Again, Elisha sent his servant—this time to invite her to come to his room. Thinking their conversation had ended, she suddenly heard a knock at the door. Opening the door, she was surprised to see Gehazi

19

standing there saying, "Elisha would like to see you." She accompanied Gehazi to the chamber and stood in the doorway. By the Spirit, Elisha had already seen her pregnant, witnessed the labor pains, and seen the birth of her son. The only thing left for him to do was to prophesy the son's birth. Elisha told her that according to the time of life, she would embrace her son: *"And he said, about this season, according to the time of life, thou shalt embrace a son.* **And she said, Nay, my lord, thou man of God, do not lie unto thine handmaid.***"* (2 Kings 4:16)

SUBJECT MATTER OF THOUGHT

Imagine how she must have felt, hearing the prophet's words *"according to the time of life."* His words may have seemed meaningless to her because she had already lived through many "life seasons" without a child.

"Guard your heart [mind] above all else, for it determines the course of your life." (Proverbs 4:23 NLT)

Thinking in the flesh, she saw him as a man playing with her emotions.

She was challenged to regain her confidence in Elisha. Remember, just a few days earlier, she told her husband, "I believe him to be a holy man of God." However, after hearing him say that she would have a son, her perception of him changed. Thinking in the flesh, she saw him as a man playing with her emotions. Why would he mock her with such an impossible promise? Why would he lie to her after all she had done for him, knowing that she was without children and that for her and her husband, the time for having children had passed?

Your "subject matter of thought" will make or break you. This I know! If you think you can't do something, you are right, but only because your words convince you. Likewise, when you say that God will not answer your prayers, again you are right, but only because of your lack of faith.

"He could not do any miracles there, except lay his hands on a few sick people and heal them. And he was amazed at their lack of faith." (Mark 6:5-6 NIV)

The past hurts that you are holding in your heart weaken your faith, causing you to doubt and reject God's promises. I ask you, would your response have been any different than hers? Is your faith strong enough to believe God can create in her a child? What do you believe concerning her miracle or for that matter, what about your own dreams, your desires, and miracles? Are you convinced, because of the time you have spent waiting, that your moment has passed? Has time caused you to quit believing in your miracle, or could it be that you have just given up? Shame on you! God has an awesome plan for you to give you hope and a future.

*"For I know the plans I have for you, declares the LORD, plans to prosper you and not to harm you, **plans to give you hope and a future.**"* (Jeremiah 29:11 NIV)

When I think of how she considered the words of life spoken by the prophet, I am reminded of when I was at Baptist Hospital in Pensacola, Florida, with my pastor. I was serving as his associate at the time. I loved visiting with him. I especially liked learning from him as he ministered to people in their needs and sorrows.

I recall one day, meeting with Harold's family when the doctor entered the waiting room. The room got very quiet as he asked for Harold's family. Someone answered, "Yes. Everyone is here." The doctor then turned his attention to Harold's wife, saying: "We have done everything we can for your husband. I am sorry to tell you that there is nothing else we can do." After the doctor left, my pastor continued speaking words of comfort to the families. Some were weeping, others hugging; their cries could be heard down the hallway.

Finally, my pastor told the family that we had to leave but to please know we were just a phone call away. I knew the next thing he would do was to pray for the family. Sure enough, he said, "We would like to pray with you." As I bowed my head, he said: "Brother Leggett, would you lead us in prayer?"

The fact that he asked me to pray did not surprise me, but what did take me by surprise was what I heard God say. I found myself considering God's words, just as the Shunammite woman had done. I raised my head, looking to my pastor and then scanning each face in the waiting room. God repeated His words a second time: "Harold will not die. He shall live." In all my years of ministry, this moment challenged me like no other.

What to do? Should I let the fear of failure keep me from speaking words of life over Harold and his family or should I trust God? By this time, my flesh had crawled up in a corner screaming: "Don't be foolish! Just say a short prayer and let's get out of here, do you hear me? Hello? Come on man, just pray and leave!"

*"Watch and pray so that you will not fall into temptation. The spirit is willing, **but the flesh is weak.**"* (Matthew 26:41 NIV)

I was tempted to close in prayer and leave. Besides, I was the only one who heard God speak, but the Holy Spirit encouraged me to speak the Lord's word with boldness—to prophesy that Harold would make a full recovery. I was called to speak words that would give God all the glory.

So, there I went: "Everyone, I have some news. God has spoken. Harold will not die. He will make a full recovery, so please join me as we pray together the prayer of life. Let us celebrate what God has done and what He is going to do, giving Him thanks for healing Harold." Many agreed. Others were unsure of what had just happened. Thanks be to God, Harold made a complete recovery, returned to church, and took his place back in the church choir. Hallelujah!

You might ask, were you scared? YOU BET I WAS, in my flesh, but in the Spirit, I was at peace. *"Death and life are in the power of the tongue, and those who love it will eat its fruit."* (Proverbs 18:21 NKJV) So, I encourage you to always speak LIFE.

THE "CAN'T DO'S" OF LIFE

Most of us were told, and our minds were programmed as children, according to the laws of the **"cannot do's."** For many of you, these words are still imprinted in your mind, limiting what you can do today. Believe me, I know my parents used the "cannot do's," and I thank God they did. *"Train up a child in the way he should go and when he is old, he will not depart from it."* (Proverbs 22:6)

However, the enemy of your soul will twist what you learned as a child—that which was intended for your good—and he will try to convince you that the "cannot do's" also apply to your faith: you cannot have God's promises and you cannot have the desires of your heart.

Most likely, you still hear: "Do not touch that, you cannot do that, you cannot have that, or leave that alone," and of course, your enemy tells you that miracles are not for today. Well, tell him, "Really! Not in my Father's Kingdom! All things are possible for me!"

God's Promise: The "CAN DO's"

Let God renew your mind—your "subject matter of thought." Pray this powerful prayer: "God, I believe that with You, I can do all things. I believe all things are possible for me. I will not be indecisive, nor will I doubt, for now I know in Christ, I CAN DO ALL THINGS. Amen."

"I can do all things through Christ which strengthened me." (Philippians 4:13) ***"Jesus said unto him, if thou canst believe, all things are possible to him that believeth."*** (Mark 9:23)

RENEWED TO BELIEVE AND PURSUE

Renew your mind to believe and to pursue your dreams, those that once seemed impossible. Pursue the desires of your heart with the confidence of knowing that all things are possible for you through Christ Jesus who strengthens you.

"And be not conformed to this world: but be ye transformed by the renewing of your mind." (Romans 12:2)

Now is the time for you to pursue your dreams, your desires, and your miracles. This is your "I Can Do" season.

"And he said, **about this season,** *according to the time of life, thou shalt embrace a son. And she said, Nay, my lord, thou man of God, do not lie unto thine handmaid."* (2 Kings 4:16)

This season of her life started out doubting the man of God, even though the first phase of God's promise—conception—was complete. As we all know, during the early months of pregnancy, the mother experiences very little, if any, change to her body. Most mothers don't know they are pregnant for weeks, and some mothers may not know for months, even though the miracle of life is already there. *"And the woman conceived."* (2 Kings 4:17)

I can only imagine her state of mind as the days turned into weeks and the weeks turned into months, with no physical change to her body. If she was not careful, her sight and emotions might have caused her to doubt that she was pregnant, convincing her that the man of God indeed lied to her.

"For we walk by faith, not by sight." (2 Corinthians 5:7)

Walking by faith is a lot more fun than walking by sight.

Walking by faith is a lot more fun than walking by sight. I think we can agree that when the promised son moved in her womb, every negative word she spoke and thought about the man of God rushed through her memory. She now realized that he truly prophesied about her son's birth. Her faith was restored and stronger than ever—this time unshakable, as we will soon see. So it is with you. Your dreams and desires are first conceived in your mind. You see little change at first but remember that your dreams and desires will be complete in God's time, as was the birth of the Shunammite woman's son.

We all have experienced times when we doubted ourselves, our dreams, desires—even times when we doubted if God Himself would answer our prayers. In these times, you need to pray, "God, please forgive me for doubting you. Renew within me the power to believe and increase my faith. Amen." Now the Shunammite woman realized that God had all the resources and power she would ever need. And so it is with you: God is your source. He will supply all your needs and power.

"That he would grant you, according to the riches of his glory, to be strengthened with might by his spirit in the inner man." (Ephesians 3:16)

As you pursue your dreams, you are to fear nothing and no one. God will open doors for you that are impossible to open. Your season of open doors is just a prayer away. Let the Holy Spirit Himself guide you to your open doors. Hallelujah!

He that hath an ear, let him hear what the spirit saith unto the churches. And to the angel of the church in Philadelphia write, these things saith he that is holy, he that is true, he that hath the key of David, he that openeth, and no man shutteth; shutteth, and no man openeth. (Revelation 3:6-7)

While we are on the topic of opened and closed doors, I'd like to tell you of a time when I was driving through the state of Alabama. I hope my testimony will encourage you to obey God when you hear Him asking you to do something that seems impossible.

LEARNING TO BELIEVE AND ACT

When you "walk by faith, not by sight," you will encounter many of God's challenges.

Believe: You must learn to trust Him.

Act: Do not allow what people say or what you see to influence you in a negative way, weakening your faith. Simply act and receive your miracle.

After driving for several hours, it was time for me to take a break, stretch my legs, and grab a bite to eat. When I came to the next town, I found a mom-and-pop restaurant. To my delight, they served fried chicken like mom cooked. While eating dinner, I noticed a young couple enter the restaurant. After I finished my meal and while paying at the counter near the front door, the Lord told me to speak to the couple the words that He would give me.

Being tired from the road trip, I decided to drive home instead and walked out to the parking lot. God has a way of parking you in the right place. As I sat in my car, I could see the young couple through the front window of the restaurant. Again, God spoke. This time, I immediately got out of my car and walked back into the restaurant to where they were seated. I asked if I could sit and talk with them, and they said "yes."

"For to one is given by the spirit the word of wisdom; to another the word of knowledge by the same spirit." (1 Corinthians 12:8-9)

I started by saying that God had given me the word of knowledge concerning them, but first, I said, "I am not from here. I am driving home from a minister's conference I attended this week. I live and pastor New Vision Worship Center in Milton, Florida." After our casual introduction, I began sharing the words from God: "The door that has closed on your ministry, God Himself closed it for your good. Men are powerless to open or close doors in God's kingdom. This is not the end of your ministry. God is moving you to a new place where you can use the gifts He has given you. Your ministry is bigger than you can even imagine."

"Sometimes God closes doors because it's time to move forward. He knows you will not move unless your circumstances force you. Trust the transition; God's got you!" —Christine Caine

The young man began weeping, placing his face in his hands, and leaning on the table. I continued to speak as the Spirit urged me. Suddenly the wife said, "You have no idea what you have done for us!" I replied, "You are right. Really, I do not. I am just obeying God." She continued: "We are youth pastors. Unknown to us, the church board decided that we were no longer needed, so they let us go." I said, "Well, I have never met you nor do I know anything about your ministry, but this I do know: God closed this door because He has a better plan for you. He released you. Not the church board."

God closes one door—to open another.

Your "subject matter of thought" will make you a victim or a winner.

Their sadness turned into unspeakable joy as they realized it was God who closed the door so that He could open a new one for their benefit. Suddenly their "subject matter of thought" (their mindset) changed from depressing thoughts regarding the board's actions, to knowing they were in God's perfect will and plan. They were thankful and thrilled about the possibility of a new beginning—a new assignment—and thankful that I had heard and obeyed God. After we chatted awhile longer, we prayed, and then I headed home. Your "subject matter of thought" will make you a victim or a winner. If God be for you, who can be against you!

"And we know that all things work together for good to them that love God, to them who are the called according to His purpose." (Romans 8:28)

Throughout life, you will experience many seasons, and in each, you must learn to accept God's purpose and plan as He closes and opens doors. In your personal life, your ministry, your job (or whatever), when God closes or opens doors, it is always for your best. Do not force open a door that God has closed.

Please take time to write your personal testimony of how God has closed or opened doors in your life, using the page at the end of this chapter. You just read one of my experiences, where God opened a door to minister the "gift of knowledge," revealing things about this precious couple whom I had just met. Only by hearing God could I have known about their situation in order to speak to them words of comfort and hope. What are the chances of my driving into a strange town and stopping at the exact restaurant where this young couple later came to have dinner? What are the odds of that happening?

You may be thinking, "God has never spoken to me," but most likely He has. After reading the Shunammite woman's story years ago, it undeniably strengthened my faith, giving me the courage to act when I hear God speak. My prayer for you is that your faith will increase to the point that you will have a new awareness of the Holy Spirit who will help you accept every opportunity that comes your way to minister. Starting today, listen for God's small, still voice. As He speaks to you, follow His instructions.

"My sheep hear my voice, and I know them." (John 10:27)

SUBSTANCE: SUBJECT MATTER OF THOUGHT

Finally, brethren, whatsoever things are true, whatsoever things are honest, whatsoever things are just, whatsoever thing are pure, whatsoever things are lovely, whatsoever things are of a good report; if there be any virtue, and if there be any praise, think on these things. (Philippians 4:8)

"Your positive action combined with positive thinking results in success."
—Shiv Khera

NOTES:

3: HOPE

*"Now faith is the substance of things **hoped** for and the evidence of things not seen."* (Hebrews 11:1)

"Hope": The feeling that what is wanted can be had or that events will turn out for the best.

"And when he had taken him, and brought him to his mother, he sat on her knee till noon, then died." (2 Kings 4:20)

In the Scriptures, God lets us celebrate with the Shunammite father as his son becomes a man, ready to join the workforce. However, the celebration is short-lived. Soon after reaching the field, his son becomes sick, crying to his father that his head hurts. His father—believing it to be a nagging headache, sends him home. One of the young men takes him to his mother, leaves him with her, and returns to the field. She holds the boy on her knee, hoping his headache will subside, but he dies.

LIFE CAN CHANGE WITHOUT WARNING.

OPEN YOUR HEART, AND INVITE GOD INTO EVERY CIR-CUMSTANCE BECAUSE WHEN GOD ENTERS THE SCENE, MIRACLES HAPPEN. *—Spiritual Inspiration*

When faced with a crisis, there is one thing you must do and that is to seek the Lord. In your prayers you will find the power to defeat the fear that has gripped you, raising you to the next level of hope where you know everything will turn out for the best. *"I sought the Lord, and he heard me, and delivered me from all my fears."* (Psalm 34:4)

Now, you may be sitting there thinking that there is no crisis in sight. Your life is better than good, it is great. I totally understand. As I sit here, everything in my life is going great. This might continue for years, but then without warning a day comes that changes everything. Being unprepared spiritually could ruin your life.

PREPARE FOR THE UNSEEN EVENTS.

You must start preparing today for the unseen trials you will encounter tomorrow.

You buy automobile insurance, hoping you will never have to use it. You pay premiums for years without a claim, sometimes thinking it is a waste of time and money. Then without warning, someone runs through a red light. With no time to react, you crash. When the state trooper shows up, his first question is always the same: "Can I see your driver's license and proof of insurance?" What a relief when you have both! Thank God you are prepared for the unseen. And so it is with your faith. You must start preparing today for the unseen trials you will encounter tomorrow. The Shunammite woman faced a life-changing event, hoping it would turn out for the best. The only way this could happen was by her faith and her belief in God and His prophet Elisha.

"The hope that God has provided for you is not merely a wish. Neither is it dependent on other people, possessions, or circumstances for its validity. Instead, biblical hope is an application of your faith that supplies a confident expectation in God's fulfillment of His promises. Coupled with faith and love, hope is part of the abiding characteristics in a believer's life." —John C. Broger

"And not only so, but we glory in tribulations also: knowing that tribulation worked patience; and patience, experience; and experience, hope." (Romans 5:3-4)

PATIENCE—EXPERIENCE—HOPE

With trials also come feelings of hopelessness. If you are not careful, these feelings can overwhelm you. While you wait for your miracle, patience is very important. You must trust that God is working everything out, even when it looks impossible. Being impatient has stopped many individuals from receiving their miracles. One thing I can guarantee, if you start doubting God, your miracle will never happen. Speak life over whatever you need—declare it to be so. SPEAK LIFE!

*"Your tongue has the power of **life and death,** and those who love it will eat its fruit."* (Proverbs 18:21)

My prayer is that this book launches you into a new awareness of the Holy Spirit and God's purpose for your life so that you find your place in the Body of Christ, where God will *"endue you with power from on high"* and with supernatural faith. He will give you the boldness to declare things and to experience miracles in this physical world that surpass all known human and natural powers, each manifesting before your eyes. The only explanation will be, "GOD DID IT!" Come on, someone shout to the Lord!!!

"But now God has set the members, each one of them, in the body just as He pleased." (1 Corinthians 12:18)

GOD PLACED YOU WHERE IT PLEASED HIM!

God created you for such a time as this and placed within you a longing to have a personal relationship with Him—just as He did for the Shunammite woman. He wishes for you to work in the gifts of the Spirit. He never intended for only a few people to have these gifts. His intent is for the whole Body of Christ—each one of us—to work in these gifts with boldness.

You will find hope in knowing that you can receive these gifts

> *For to one is given by the Spirit the **word of wisdom;** to another the **word of knowledge** To another **faith,** to another the **gifts of healing,** To another the **working of miracles;** to another **prophecy;** to another **discerning of spirits;** to another **diverse kinds of tongues;** to another the **interpretation of tongues;** But all these worketh that one and the selfsame Spirit, **dividing to every man severally as he will.*** (1 Corinthians 12:8-11)

HOPE IS KNOWING GOD EQUIPS YOU FOR THE BATTLE.

God is no respecter of persons. He will give you supernatural power, supernatural faith, and supernatural courage to do whatever He has called you to do—the same power, faith, and courage he gave to the Shunammite woman. As God raised her up in her generation, He is raising you up in this generation to be great men and women of fearless faith. God is preparing you to be part of the awesome assembly called the Church, known as the Body of Christ. He has set before you his Great Commission to spread the word of salvation, to cast out devils, to heal the sick.

> *And these signs shall follow them that believe; In my name shall they cast out devils; they shall speak with new tongues; They shall take up serpents; and if they drink any deadly thing, it shall not hurt them; **they shall lay hands on the sick, and they shall recover.***
> (Mark 16:17-18)

SUPERNATURAL FAITH

The Shunammite woman, with the boldness of a warrior, accepted her mission, and she confronted her enemy Death with the attitude that nothing and no one would get in the way of her son's miracle. Think what would happen if we, the members of His Church around the world, show up Sunday mornings with that kind of faith, each shouting, "Today, nothing shall get in the way of my miracle! This day I will receive my miracle!"

HOPE—FAITH—WORKS

As you read this book, I know God will increase your faith as the Holy Spirit speaks to you words of encouragement. God has chosen you as His vessel and has given you permission and the confidence to call on His name for healing, deliverance, salvation, and yes, the authority to cast out demons. When you totally surrender your life to God, *"Then you will call into existence the things that do not exist. Hallelujah!"*

*"[I]t is written, 'I have made you the father of many nations'—in the presence of the God in whom he believed, who gives life to the dead and **calls into existence the things that do not exist.***" (Romans 4:17 ESV)

You may ask yourself, "How can I have that kind of faith?" God gives every born-again believer a measure of faith. Now, use the faith God has given you to speak to the things that are not, as if they are. You have God's permission to speak life into every situation.

Elisha's bed became her Altar.

"And she went up and laid him on the bed of the man of God, and shut the door upon him, and went out." (2 Kings 4:21)

Without warning, her day turned to darkness. The subject matter of her mind suddenly changed from her normal daily routine of being a wife and mother—preparing for her husband's and her son's return home from the fields—to being a parent who suddenly lost her child. This day did not turn out as expected.

"Yet what we suffer now is nothing compared to the glory he will reveal to us later." (Romans 8:18 NLT)

I feel her pain and understand her grief as she faced this ordeal, but this day was like no other. This day, she faced the valley of the shadow of death—a place that few of us have physically or spiritually experienced. She may have thought, "What can I do?" Remember her first test when Elisha announced the birth of her son? Her unbelief caused her to reject his words, but this time things were different. This time, she approached her trial with a positive attitude. As she prepared for her trip, she believed for a good report. She believed God would change His mind and raise her son back to life.

"Yea, though I walk through the valley of the shadow of death, I will fear no evil: for thou art with me; thy rod and staff they comfort me." (Psalm 23:4)

Do you think it is possible to change God's mind?

Do you think it is possible to change God's mind? What must she do to change His mind? For that matter, has God ever changed His mind? I remember as a child hearing people say that if God said it, that settles it. The end.

In 2 Kings, King Hezekiah was sick unto death when the prophet Isaiah stopped by to visit (2 Kings 20:1-11). For most Christians who are deathly ill, the first person they call is their pastor or the leader of a prayer team. You would think that Isaiah's visiting the king was a good thing, but his visit was not to comfort the king. He was sent by God to deliver a warning: **"Set thine house in order; for thou shalt die, and not live."** God said it, and that settles it. The end, right?

"I beseech thee O Lord, remember now how I have walked before thee in truth and with a perfect heart, and have done that which is good in thy sight. And Hezekiah wept sore." (2 Kings 20:3)

I believe it would have been settled, but the king's reaction to Isaiah's message changed everything. He immediately turned to the wailing wall that represented His God "Jehovah Rophe—My Healer." The king's hope was not in the prophet. His hope was in his God. As the prophet left the palace, Hezekiah prayed.

"For I know the plans I have for you," declares the Lord, "plans to prosper you and not to harm you, plans to give you HOPE and a future." (Jeremiah 29:11)

HOPING TO CHANGE GOD'S MIND

I notice this about his prayer: the king did not plead for his life. His main concern was, "What did I do wrong? How did I fail my God?" In his prayer, he reminded God how he walked with a perfect heart. As he wept, he reminded God of all the good things he had done. Being moved by Hezekiah's tears and prayer, God sent Isaiah back to the king's palace.

Turn again, and tell Hezekiah the captain of my people, thus saith the Lord, the God of David thy father, I have heard thy prayer, I have seen thy tears: behold I will heal thee: on the third day thou shalt go up unto the house of the Lord. (2 Kings 20:5)

The king looked up with tear-stained eyes, seeing the prophet once again standing in the palace. This time he received great news. Isaiah said, *"God heard your prayers and has seen your tears. He will heal you, plus extend your life and give you victory over the King of Assyria."*

"And I will add unto thy days fifteen years; and I will deliver thee and this city out of the hand of the king of Assyria." (2 Kings 20:6)

As my mother would say, "Prayer changes things." The king received his healing, and God added fifteen years to his life. God also delivered him and his city out of the hands of his enemy. Remember, God is moved by your prayers and tears.

HOPE IN KNOWING THAT PRAYER WILL CHANGE GOD'S MIND.

Before leaving her home, she carried her son to Elisha's room—the same room she built and dedicated to God years earlier—laying him on the Prophet's bed and turning it into her altar. I imagine that before leaving the chamber, she spent time in prayer calling on her God.

The Shunammite's battle started at the altar. Hezekiah's prayer and his tears moved God to compassion. What better place for you to start than at the altar in prayer? There are times when you need to worship God with your prayer. You need a special place to pray. Sometimes you need to kneel when praying. Why? It feels awesome when you kneel to God. Dedicate a time to pray each day. You may think prayer is not that important. Some people only pray when they need something from God. What is your thought on fasting and prayer? When was your last fast? What was the reason? Is fasting for today? Is fasting necessary to have your prayers answered?

Then came the disciples to Jesus apart, and said, Why could not we cast him out? And Jesus said unto them, Because of your unbelief: for verily I say unto you, If ye have faith as a grain of mustard seed, ye shall say unto this mountain, Remove hence to yonder place; and it shall remove; and nothing shall be impossible unto you. Howbeit this kind goeth not out but by prayer and fasting. (Matthew 17:19-21)

At the end of this chapter, you will find a page provided for notes. Write down your last fast and why you were fasting. It is good to keep records of your prayers. Amen.

I recall growing up in Beulah, Florida, a small rural community where most of our friends lived on small farms. We were on summer vacation from school when my mom decided to visit one of our neighbors. After arriving, my brothers, our friend, and I were playing cowboys with our cap guns in their home. We asked permission to go outside. Our mothers said we could but warned us to stay away from the horses in the corral.

Without warning, the horse kicked, and his hoof caught Wayne just above his eye, lifting him into the air.

Outside, playing hide-and-seek, we found ourselves near the corral, climbing up on the four-rail ranch fence and petting and feeding the horses from outside the corral. Disregarding our mother's warning, we soon climbed over the fence into the corral with the horses. All but one horse remained calm. As it began trotting away, my brother, Wayne, chased after him. Without warning, the horse kicked, and his hoof caught Wayne just above his eye, lifting him into the air. When he hit the ground, he laid motionless.

I ran to my brother; what I saw and heard frightened me. Blood was running down his face onto the ground, and he was having difficulty breathing. I immediately tried to pick him up, but fear weakened me. I could not lift him through the fence, so I called out to my mother. Hearing me, she came running to the corral. When she saw Wayne in my arms, she helped me put him into our car, and she started driving to the nearest hospital 30 miles away in Pensacola, Florida.

She was driving extremely fast and recklessly, all the while reminding us to pray for Wayne. As I prayed, I also asked God to keep us safe. What happened next was God's sovereignty and protection: the engine died, and the car coasted to a stop in the small town of Ensley. Mother found a white cloth, and I watched as she tied it to the antenna. I didn't understand why she did that, but it seemed like less than a minute when a man driving by noticed the cloth and stopped to give assistance. Mother explained to him what had happened. Seeing Wayne, he immediately put us into his pickup truck and drove us to the hospital.

Dad arrived about an hour later. The emergency room doctor met with my parents to update them on Wayne's condition. He explained that his condition was critical and his breathing was limited. He had placed Wayne on a ventilator, trying to stabilize him and would not do surgery that night. "In his condition, he may not survive the surgery," he said, then encouraged my parents to get some rest.

Local radio and TV stations featured Wayne's story on the evening news. Many ministers came to the hospital to pray for Wayne and for our family. I still recall Mother telling us about one young minister who came to the waiting room. He asked permission to pray for Wayne. Mother told us that he prayed with such power and confidence—not with loud speech, but with a calmness about him, like he knew God was hearing every word. He left her with a sense of hope.

"There is surely a future hope for you, and your hope will not be cut off." (Proverbs 23:18 NIV)

EXPERIENCE OF HOPE

That night, Mother experienced God's Spirit like never before. A calmness and peace came over her as God's Spirit moved across the waiting room. She described it as a breath of fresh air moving through the hospital. At that very moment, she knew Wayne would be alright. *It shall be well.* He made it through the night and through the surgery. I know it was the prayers of many, including the prayers of hope from the young preacher. After the surgery, his doctor said that most likely, Wayne would have recurring seizures throughout his life. God said "no" to those words. He never had a seizure. He grew up to have a beautiful family and grandchildren. To God be the glory! I am thankful for a mother who realized the importance of getting to the hospital in a timely manner, parents who taught their children to pray, all the ministers who came to the hospital to spend time with our family in prayer, and the doctors and medical staff.

As this young minister prayed words over Wayne with confidence, the Shunammite woman spoke words of life over her son without hesitating and without disbelief. This time, she would not let anything get in her way. Her mission was clear: to remind God of His promise. Her declaration: "IT SHALL BE WELL."

*"And he said, wherefore wilt thou go to him today? It is neither new moon, nor sabbath. And she said, **it shall be well.** "* (2 Kings 4:23)

By faith, she left her son's lifeless body on Elisha's bed, knowing God would restore her son. When I read the Bible, I imagine each character. I know God has a purpose for each one. If He took time to write about them, we should take time to learn about them and their worth to us, the readers.

The bottom line is this: no matter how many people God sends to help you, or how many resources He supplies, if you let the skeptics with their negative thinking discourage you, you will never get to the place God has for you. Separate yourself from the naysayers. Seek those whom God has sent to help you who are supportive of your vision. Remember, it is your vision and miracle, so let nothing stand in your way.

*"Now the God of **Hope** fill you with all joy and peace in believing, that ye may abound in **Hope,** through the power of the Holy Ghost."* (Romans 15:13)

NOTES:

_____

_____

_____

_____

_____

_____

_____

_____

_____

_____

_____

_____

_____

_____

_____

_____

_____

_____

_____

_____

_____

_____

_____

_____

_____

_____

_____

_____

4: THAT I MAY RUN

*"And she called unto her husband, and said, send me, one of the young men, and one of the asses, **that I may run to the man of God,** and come again."* (2 Kings 4:22)

RUN WITH STRENGTH, DISCIPLINE, AND PATIENCE.

*"But they that wait upon the Lord shall renew their strength; they shall mount up with wings as eagles; **they shall run and not be weary; and they shall walk, and not faint."*** (Isaiah 40:31)

"Running to the man of God" is an interesting concept. During my 34 years in ministry, most people whom I had the privilege of meeting were running from God, but this great woman, being led by the Spirit, ran toward the man of God. She was totally convinced that her God would bring her son back to life, but first she embarked on a marathon. She started in her hometown of Shunem, travelled to Mount Carmel, then returned with Elisha.

It took nine hours to reach the base of Mount Carmel, which is 24 miles in length, 5 miles wide, and 1,724 feet high. The trip was reason enough for her to accept the hand that life had dealt her. Most would say that there was nothing she could do. Even so, she was not willing to face the obvious, and her faith told her to accept nothing less than the resurrection of her son.

Knowing that God could be reached every day, she believed He would answer her prayers with mercy. *"You shall make two cherubim of gold, make them of hammered work at the two ends of the **mercy seat.**"* (Exodus 25:18)

INMATE FINDS MERCY

A friend asked me if I would go with him to Holman Correctional Facility in Atmore, Alabama. Holman is the facility that carries out all executions for death row inmates in the state of Alabama and is perhaps one of the most feared facilities to be incarcerated in because it is the "last stop" for many inmates. This facility was the topic of a documentary called *Lockup,* which premiered in 2006. The documentary covered Holman's notorious reputation as the most violent prison in all of Alabama.

The warden gave our ministry team permission to grill hamburgers for the correction officers, staff, and inmates onsite. I was invited as guest speaker during the event—what a blessing to have this opportunity. Our team, made up of several churches and two Gospel quartets, left early Saturday morning from Pace, Florida, driving fifty-seven miles to Holman Corrections.

Upon arriving, we were escorted to a multipurpose room where members of the security searched us, our vehicles, our barbecue grills, and the sound equipment before allowing us to enter the main compound. Once inside, our work began. We soon encountered a ten-foot, chain-link fence for the safety of our volunteers and musicians. Our team of servers, including myself, moved beyond the chain-link fence to the prison yard, where we set up the buffet tables.

The musicians began tuning their instruments and testing the microphones as the smell of hamburgers cooking on the grills filled the air. The inmates began to gather near the fence as they started lining up for the meal. We set out trays of potato salad, baked beans, and desserts.

In a very short time, we served over one hundred inmates. Each of them was thankful and polite, but there was one who was listening to his transistor radio as he made his way through the buffet line, shouting profanity and being unruly. I thought that maybe his football team was losing—it was that time of year. As he drew closer, God gave me words to speak to him. It was my first time in a prison yard with hundreds of inmates. To single out one of them and speak words that he may not receive well made me nervous, but the Spirit reminded me of God's promise: ***"He will never leave nor forsake you."*** Learn to trust Him and do what He asks of you.

More and more, as I watched the inmates receive their trays, the Holy Spirit became my comfort. Soon, the inmate was standing in front of me. His tray was in his left hand and the radio was in his right, pressed to his ear. He was expecting a dessert. I placed the dessert on his tray, and then

> If you continue on the path you have chosen, there will come a time when He will not answer you.

I quickly removed it. He immediately dropped the hand with the radio and without saying a word just stared at me. Now having his attention, I said, "God told me to tell you, to stop running from and playing games with Him because you know better. He also said when you hear my words you will know they are from Him. If you continue on the path you have chosen, there will come a time when He will not answer you. This is your day to repent and start obeying Him." And I would say to you, the reader, this is your day as well.

"For he saith, I have heard thee in a time accepted, and in the day of salvation have I succoured thee: behold, now is the accepted time; behold, now is the day of salvation." (2 Corinthians 6:2)

Then I gave him the dessert, and he walked away with a perplexed look on his face. He never said a word as he blended in with the other white jumpsuits in the prison yard. After feeding everyone, we loaded the trucks and trailers for our trip home, and it was time for the evening chapel service.

INMATE ANSWERED THE CALL

As I entered the chapel with our ministry team, it was standing room only. I noticed the inmate was sitting in the back pew. We made eye contact but did not speak. The inmates had their own worship team and did an awesome job. After the worship service, I brought the message, and as I gave the altar call, he ran to the altar, falling on his knees weeping. Many were at the altar praying.

"Thank God! Today I repented, giving my life back to Him."

While making my way to him, he stood up, and before I knew what was happening, his arms were around me, lifting me up on my toes. He said, "We have a lot of preachers come to this prison, but none ever spoke to me like you did today. You're right. I have been playing games with God. I'm not trying to justify my actions, but in prison for your own protection, you must act and be tough. But on the inside, my spirit was weak and dying. I had lost all my joy and peace. I knew God was not pleased with what I had become, knowing I was both physically and spiritually in prison. Thank you for obeying God. The moment you began speaking, I received His words and felt Him release the enemy's hold that he had on me for years. Thank God! Today I repented, giving my life back to Him."

What he said next made me smile: "I wish you would have waited until after lunch to share God's warning because after hearing what you had to say, I just sat with the food on my lap. Eating was not on my mind. My stomach felt the size of my fist. All I could think about was the altar."

The next month, our ministry team returned to Holman. Again we met, and to my joy, I noticed he had drawn a fish on his jumpsuit. Another name written down in glory. When I was at Holman Prison watching the inmate run to the altar, God placed within me the spirit to run when He calls. We must run in the spirit to the father.

The inmate was my first salvation behind the prison walls. Two years later, I started New Vision Jail Ministry. I am currently serving as Senior Chaplain for New Vision Jail Ministries at Escambia County Corrections in Pensacola, Florida, and have been serving in that capacity for the past twenty-eight years with the help of my ministry team—120 strong. I have baptized over 4,000 inmates.

It is important that we learn from these examples: the inmate running to the altar and the Shunammite woman running to God's prophet Elisha. The word tells us, when we "draw nigh to God, he will draw nigh to us."

"Know ye not that they which run in a race run all, but one receives the prize? **So run, that ye may obtain.***"* (1 Corinthians 9:24)

The Shunammite woman ran that she might obtain the prize. Can you hear the urgency in her voice as she called out to her husband: "Send me a young man and one of the asses that I may run to the man of God?" I do not know why she kept their son's condition from her husband. Maybe she did not want to defend her reasoning, knowing that she had very little time to waste.

STARTING AT THE ALTAR?

"You did run well: who did hinder you that ye should not obey the truth?" (Galatians 5:7)

Personally, I have never run a marathon. I am a member of the *"Stand Still, and See the Salvation of the Lord Club."* Can I get a witness? There are many types of marathons: the 5K/three-mile (one of the most popular), the 10K mid-distance, and the 21K/half marathon (the first of the long-distance races). The most challenging marathon—yet the shortest of all marathons for the unsaved—starts in the church pew and ends a few feet away at the altar. Sadly, many who enter this race will not finish it. The first leg begins on Sunday mornings during worship service. The enemy of your soul, satan, is known as *"the thief cometh not, but for to steal, and to kill, and to destroy."* (John 10:10) His goal is to convince you that you really don't need this salvation, saying that all you need is to make it through the song service, holding back tears and hoping that no one notices. The second leg is more challenging. The pastor's message brings conviction, and you feel God's Spirit drawing you. Your heart is telling you to go down to the altar, but you are still not willing to give up your lifestyle. You hold even tighter. The last and most difficult leg is the altar call and will take all the strength you have to refuse God's love and forgiveness. You nervously watch the worship leader walk to the podium. The pastor asks everyone to stand, while the organist plays "Nothing but the Blood of Jesus." Again, you tightly grip the pew in front of you. Finally, the organist stops playing. The pastor closes with prayer. Relieved that it is over, you release the pew, unchanged. You do not want to lose this race, but many will. Does this sound familiar? If you're thinking, what must you do to be saved, the answer is simple:

> *That if thou shalt confess with thy mouth the Lord Jesus, and shalt believe in thine heart that God hath raised him from the dead, thou shalt be saved. For with the heart man believeth unto righteousness; and with the mouth confession is made unto salvation.*
> (Romans 10:9-10)

Prayer: "Jesus I confess with my mouth that you are Lord, and I believe with my heart that God raised you from the dead. Please forgive me of my sins. Come into my heart. I will serve you as my Lord and Savior. Amen"

Paul said, *"I have finished the race."* (2 Timothy 4:7 NIV) This is a message of hope to all Christians and unsaved alike who are running the race. This is the hope. You can finish the race. So, run to win. Amen!

JOIN THE TEAM.

First thing, ask God, "Is my heart strong enough to finish?" I thought that my heart was in good condition. I had never experienced chest pain or shortness of breath, but that changed while fishing with my wife Radena at Fort Pickens in Pensacola. The Spanish Mackerel were plentiful around the pier, and I had already caught several. Needing more bait, I grabbed my bait net, casting it over a school of bait fish. Suddenly, a sharp pain shot from my back to my chest. I didn't tell my wife at first, waiting for it to subside before trying to pull in the net. As I tried a second time, the pain hit me again, and this time it took my breath away. Radena noticed I was having trouble with the net and asked if I was alright. I said, "No, we need to go to the hospital."

After arriving at the emergency room, one of the cardiologists entered my room. He checked my vitals, and I thought he was going to say, "Everything looks good; you can go home." Instead, he said, "After looking at your angiogram, you have three blocked vessels near your heart. We have scheduled triple bypass surgery on Monday morning." After my surgery, the surgeon told me that because I had decided to come to the hospital at the first sign of pain, he was able to clear the blockage without damage to the heart. He said, "You should be fine."

"My flesh and my heart faileth: but God is the strength of my heart, and my portion forever." (Psalm 73:26)

This encounter with my heart caused me to think about my spiritual heart. I know plaque blocks the arteries of the fleshly heart, and we know poor diet and lack of exercise and stress causes plaque. What blocks the arteries of a spiritual heart, making it impossible for us to run well?

"Pride goeth before destruction, and a haughty spirit before a fall." (Proverbs 16:18)

REPLACE A STONY HEART.

We know that hardening of the arteries can do serious damage to the human heart. The word tells us, we can have a stony heart, making it impossible to run well because we struggle loving those closest to us and find it difficult to even trust God. I think the plaque of a stony heart is a haughty spirit.

> Ask God to remove the stony heart, replacing it with a humble and gentle spirit.

The haughty spirit will convince you that you're running well, but the truth of the matter is that your arrogant and prideful self will cause you to fall before finishing the race. I know you want to run well, so let's fix your heart. Ask God to remove the stony heart, replacing it with a humble and gentle spirit. Learn to be compassionate and forgiving of others as you run.

"A new heart also will I give you, and a new spirit will I put within you: and will take away the stony heart out of your flesh, and I will give you a heart of flesh." (Ezekiel 36:26)

REPLACE A FEARFUL HEART.

A fearful heart has kept many of you out of the race. God says, "Run the race set before you, for I promise to be with you, and I will give you everything you need to finish, but before you can even take the first step you must overcome the fear that weakens you spiritually." God tells us to be strong and courageous, even in times when we feel weak to the point we can't lift our hands to worship,

"Fear thou not; for I am with thee: be not dismayed; for I am thy God: I will strengthen thee; yea, I will help thee; yea, I will uphold thee with the right hand of my righteousness." (Isaiah 41:10)

Be fearless! God says not to be afraid or alarmed, for you can trust that wherever He sends you, He will be with you. His blessings cover you. His mercies chase after you. When troubles come, His Spirit shall strengthen and comfort your heart. His peace He leaves with you. The word tells you the Lord is always before you. Remember, He is the One leading you. Give all your worries to Him. He will crush your fears.

RUN WITH A TRUSTING HEART.

"Trust in the Lord with all thine heart; and lean not unto thine own understanding. In all thy ways acknowledge him, and he shall direct thy paths" (Proverbs 3:5-6)

For you to run well, you must trust God with all your heart as the Shunammite woman trusted God's servant. Learn to lean on His every word and follow His directions as she did. Remember, He is your guide. *"Thomas said unto him, Lord, we know not whither thou goes; and how can we know the way? Jesus saith unto him, I am the way."* (John 14:5-6)

A trusting heart is filled with praise, knowing that He is the way. It is the Lord who makes the heart beat strong and protects the runner. Therefore, the runner's mouth should always be filled with rejoicing and songs of praise. The more you trust Him, the more you receive from Him, because you have tasted His great salvation. Therefore, you run.

Those who trust the Lord realize their hope is in Him. They accept the challenges of life, confident that God will help them conquer each one.

A trusting heart is said to be like a tree growing near a river. The hot summer days will have no effect on it because its roots have grown deep in the soil. Likewise, by faith, a trusting heart has attached itself to every promise of God, and when trials come, the heart knows God will work things out.

RUN WITH A DEVOTED HEART.

"Let your heart therefore be (devoted) perfect with the Lord our God, to walk in his statutes, and to keep his commandments, as at this day." (1 Kings 8:61)

The Shunammite woman's heart was devoted to her family and her God. As you run for the King, you must step up your game. Having a devoted heart is, for many, stepping up their game. God challenges each of us to be the best we can be. Let your mind be set on the high calling of God, knowing Christ is watching. You have joined His team. Now accept your responsibility, and that is to help the team keep the unity of faith by staying focused on the mission to become Christlike in every way.

As you run, stay focused on His will. Ask Him to search your heart. He will show you what needs to be corrected; then do whatever He asks. A devoted heart is willing to be corrected. God searches the heart with or without your permission. Men look on the outward appearance, but the Lord looks on the heart. How's your heart looking?

RUN WITH A FORGIVING HEART.

"And be ye kind one to another, tenderhearted, forgiving one another, even as God for Christ's sake hath forgiven you." (Ephesians 4:32)

So, you say you know how to forgive, but there are some people whom you have decided not to forgive. God's plan, when it comes to forgiveness, benefits both the person forgiving and the one receiving forgiveness.

Harboring unforgiveness in your heart—that's really being Christlike?

The heart is the most important part of the spiritual person. To keep it strong and clean, you must freely forgive. *"Judge not, and ye shall not be judged: Condemn not, and ye shall not be condemned: forgive, and you shall be forgiven."* (Luke 6:37)

When harboring unforgiveness, you become another person's judge, finding him unworthy of your forgiveness and putting yourself in danger of God's judgment. You condemn the person as being reprehensible, wrong, or evil. By whose standards? Your own? The word tells us, "All have sinned and come short of the glory of God." When you judge others, you place yourself in danger of God condemning you.

TO RUN STRONG: Avoid judgment, condemnation, and practice forgiveness.

NOTES:

_____

_____

_____

_____

_____

_____

_____

_____

_____

_____

_____

_____

_____

_____

_____

_____

_____

_____

_____

_____

_____

_____

_____

_____

_____

_____

_____

_____

_____

5: SLACK NOT

"Then she saddled an ass, and said to her servant, 'Drive, and go forward; **slack not thy riding for me,** *except I bid thee.'"* (2 Kings 4:24)

The Shunammite woman knew that she would likely get weary on the trip, both physically and spiritually, as she searched for the Prophet Elisha, so she instructed the young man not to slack on her behalf. Her words challenge us today not to slack as well. *"The soul of the sluggard desireth, and hath nothing: but the soul of the diligent shall be made fat."* (Proverbs 13:4) Before taking her first step, the Shunammite woman vowed to God and to her son that she would be diligent on the journey.

Think back on the day you gave your life to the Lord and how wonderful you felt knowing God forgave all your sins. Most likely, you made a vow to God. Whatever you promised Him, it was your first step on a lifelong journey to your heavenly home. Have you been diligent in keeping your promise? If not, it is not too late to fulfill your commitment to Him. Like the Shunammite woman who asked the young man to keep her focused, you need the Holy Spirit to guide you.

"When you make a vow to God, do not delay paying it. For he has no pleasure in fools; pay what you have vowed. Better not to vow than to vow and not pay." (Ecclesiastes 5:4-5) NKJV

Led by the Holy Spirit, the Shunammite woman ran with purpose while praising God for the miracles He had done and what He was going to do. She gave the young man one order: to keep encouraging her to continue and not to slack. The Scripture does not state whether she rested. If she had, would God consider the time she spent resting as slacking in her commitment to Him? She did say, "Do not slack unless I bid you." What if she took time to rest? Would it have a negative effect on her son's miracle?

Don't confuse resting with slacking. You may find yourself needing to take a break from your ministry, job, social activities, or anything you are involved in to regroup. The task before you may seem overwhelming because you have already fought many economical, spiritual, emotional, physical, and mental battles, and you find yourself exhausted. You just can't continue. What would God think if you decided to take a break in the heat of the battle?

I turned to the Scriptures to find the answer.

Does God reward us for the work we contributed prior to taking time off to rest?

I first thought of God when He created the heavens and the earth in six days. Then on the 7th day, He rested from all His work. Your critics may say, "Yeah, but God finished his work; afterward He rested." Of course, they would be correct. For those of us who have given notice to our team members in the middle of a project, saying, "I am taking time off," even knowing the team needs us, does God reward us for the work we contributed prior to taking time off to rest? Does God recognize the work someone does prior to taking a break?

I found the answer in 1 Samuel 30. Not only did God give David's men credit for their previous work, but He also defended them when the men who fought in the battle turned their anger toward those who stayed behind. This should bring peace and joy to you. Some of you have rested for weeks and months. Perhaps you are feeling embarrassed and guilty, thinking you let the team and God down. In Scripture, God assures you. You do not let others down. He will silence your critics, making sure you receive your reward as did David's men.

1 SAMUEL 30

David and his men came to the city, and behold, it burned with fire; and their wives, and their sons, and their daughters, were taken captives. And David was distressed for the people spoke of stoning him, because the soul of all the people was grieved, every man for his sons and for his daughters. (1 Samuel 30:3,6)

What just happened? While David and his men were away on the battlefield, the enemy invaded Ziklag, their hometown, burning it to the ground. They took captive their wives, children, and all their belongings, causing David's men to turn on him, ready to stone him. David did not defend himself. He called on his God for comfort and direction.

"And David enquired at the Lord, saying, 'Shall I pursue after this troop? Shall I overtake them?' Then God answered him, 'Pursue for thou shalt surely overtake them, and without fail recover all.'" (1 Samuel 30:8)

Most likely, the enemy has not burned your hometown to the ground. Even so, you can relate to David's saga, asking: "Father what should I do?"

David pursued.

"But David pursued, he and four hundred men: for two hundred abode behind, which were so faint they could not go over the brook." (1 Samuel 30:10)

David pursued with the 400 warriors who, trusting in God's promise, believed they would recover all. However, 200 men stayed behind, too fatigued to continue, knowing the promise was for those who pursued. Even so, they could not cross over the brook.

Have you ever found yourself standing spiritually and physically on the shores of life, too fatigued to cross over? Could it be that you are standing on the shores even now? That's okay. I have some news for you!

And David recovered all that the Amalekites had carried away: and David rescued his two wives. And there was nothing lacking to them, neither small nor great, neither sons nor daughters, neither spoil, nor any thing that they had taken to them: David recovered all.
(1 Samuel 30:18-19)

When God tells you to pursue, trust Him, for you shall recover all.

Take a deep breath—deeper, deeper. Now shout: ***The salvation of the Lord has come to my house! If God be for me, who can be against me!*** When friends and colleagues condemn you, hold your peace knowing that God is on your side. *"What shall we then say to these things? If God is for us, who can be against us?"* (Romans 8:31)

"And David came to the two hundred men, which were so faint that they could not follow David, whom they had made also to abide at the brook Besor: and they went forth to meet David, and to meet the people that were with him: and when David came near to the people, he saluted them." (1 Samuel 30:21)

Salute of respect

These two-hundred men had earned David's respect while fighting with him on the battlefield days before on the banks of Besor. The king knew they were men of valor and could be trusted. They were not quitters.

> *Then answered all the wicked men and men of Belial, of those that went with David, and said, because they went not with us, we will not give them ought of the spoil that we have recovered, save to every man his wife and his children, that they may lead them away, and depart.* (1 Samuel 30:22)

These were greedy men, thinking only of themselves.

> *Then said David, "Ye shall not do so, my brethren, with that which the Lord hath given us, who hath preserved us, and delivered the company that came against us into our hand. For who will hearken unto you in this matter? but as his part is that goeth down to the battle,* ***so shall his part be that tarried by the stuff: they shall part alike." And it was so from that day forward, that he made it a statute and an ordinance for Israel unto this day.*** (1 Samuel 30:23-25)

God's answer is clear. If the Shunammite woman or you rest during your trial—even in the heat of the battle—He will answer your prayers, and you shall recover all. So, now you have the answer that you have been praying for. It doesn't matter what others may say.

"But they that wait upon the Lord shall renew their strength; they shall mount up with wings as eagles; they shall run, and not be weary; and they shall walk, and not faint." (Isaiah 40:31)

You shall recover all.

I have met many people who have wished for things all their lives, only to accomplish nothing. I explain that it takes more than wishing. You must have faith and be willing to work. My dad always said, "Anything worth having is worth working for." *"Even so faith, if it hath not works, is dead, being alone."* (James 2:17)

The Bible is not a Wish Book. It is an action Book.

The Shunammite woman believed that God would restore life to her son, and she was willing to work toward that end. Maybe, during your life, you have wished for your dreams to come true, yet you are not willing to work to make these dreams happen. Are you working or just sitting in your La-Z-Boy recliner? God has been long-suffering with you. Now is the time to stop wishing for your miracles or the things that you need and start pleasing God by your faith. Prove to Him that you are willing to do whatever He requires from you.

*"But **without faith it is impossible to please** him: for he that cometh to God must believe that he is, and that he is a rewarder of them that diligently seek him."* (Hebrews 11:6)

TIME TO WORK

This I have found to be true: the only thing freely given is your salvation.

"For by grace are ye saved through faith; and that not of yourselves: it is the gift of God: Not of works lest any man should boast." (Ephesians 2:8-9) We should forever praise God for sending His Son to die on an old, rugged cross in our stead.

I encourage you to write down your dreams and visions. Use the page provided at the end of this chapter. Let the Holy Spirit guide you as you write. *"And the Lord answered me, and said, 'Write the vision, and make it plain upon tables, that he may run that read it.'"* (Habakkuk 2:2) Your vision is clear to everyone who reads it. Now, it is time to get busy working because those people who believe in you and your vision are ready to help you, but only if they see your faith through your works.

> ## Are you willing to give another person permission to question your motives when you are being complacent?

Next, you need a well-thought-out plan to help you manage your time, resulting in less slack and wasted resources. The Shunammite woman had a very clear plan. To make sure she stayed focused, she asked the young man to be her accountability partner. Are you willing to give another person permission to question your motives when you are being complacent? If this one paragraph is all you remember from my book, it will help you be successful at whatever you plan to do. You must be willing to let those who have more knowledge and experience challenge you. Here are some important challenges to consider and practice.

SLACK NOT IN YOUR GIVING.

"Will a man rob God? Yet ye have robbed me. But ye say, wherein have we robbed thee? In tithes and offerings. Ye are cursed with a curse: for ye have robbed me, even this whole nation." (Malachi 3:8-9) Ouch! You should answer God's question with a question: "Father am I robbing you?" I remember as I grew up, hearing my dad say, "What I keep from God on Sunday, satan takes on Monday." For those who pay their tithe, God promises to rebuke the devourer for their sake.

A COMMANDMENT WITH A PROMISE

In 1986, I was truly the prodigal son, returning home, physically, mentally, and spiritually. Like the Scripture says, I had journeyed into a far country. I wasted all my substance there with riotous living. For years, I did things my way. Now I had to learn to do things God's way. My first challenge came during a Sunday morning service after my wife, Radena, and I started attending church. One of the ministers walked out onto the platform, joyfully saying, "It is time to worship God with our giving."

Before the service, Radena had given me our tithe. I found myself having a tough time getting into the spirit of worship. Instead, all I could think about was our bills, especially the ones that were months overdue. We both agreed to catch up on past-due payments and pay our tithes, but that week if I gave our tithe, we would not have enough money to make it to my next payday. How many times have you thought the same thing?

The minister said, "Let us pray," and while everyone had their eyes closed and heads bowed, I took the opportunity to remove a portion of the tithe and put it in my pocket. My flesh had persuaded me that I was doing the right thing, but then I heard God's small still voice say, "Trust Me and see if I will not open the windows of heaven and pour out a blessing for you." Knowing what I should do, but still reluctant, I gave all the tithes.

> *Bring ye all the tithes into the storehouse, that there may be meat in mine house,* **and prove me now herewith, saith the Lord of hosts, if I will not open you the windows of heaven, and pour you out a blessing,** *that there shall not be room enough to receive it.* (Malachi 3:10)

After we returned home, I went out to the garage with the church service still on my mind, thinking, "How in the world will we make it to our next payday?" Soon after, Radena came to the garage to tell me someone wanted to speak with me on the phone. The caller asked if I would do a small welding project for him. When he told me what he was willing to pay, I realized it was more than double the amount of the tithe. With tears in my eyes, I told Radena what God had done. Together, we prayed, thankful for His blessings and His promise. From that day forward, we gave our tithes, and yes, we paid them with joyful hearts.

You may think that those who can afford to give larger tithes and offerings receive greater blessings, but that is not true. All God requires is the tenth. For some, their tithe could be as small as $2.00 and others it could be $2,000.00. Both are justified and will receive equal blessings. A perfect example is "the widow's mite":

> *And Jesus sat over against the treasury and beheld how the people cast money into the treasury: and many who were rich cast in much. And there came a certain poor widow, and she threw in two mites, which make a farthing. And he called unto him his disciples, and saith unto*

them, "Verily I say unto you, that this poor widow hath cast more in, than all they which have cast into the treasury: For all they did cast in of their abundance; but she of her want did cast in all that she had, even all her living." (Mark 12:41-44)

Do not allow satan or anyone to put a guilt trip on you when giving your tithe and offerings. It is between you and God: *"Every man according as he purposed in his heart, so let him give; not grudgingly, or of necessity: for God loveth a cheerful giver."* (2 Corinthians 9:7)

The Shunammite woman set the example of giving with a cheerful heart. God responded by opening the windows of heaven and pouring out blessings and miracles.

WHEN YOUR CHILDREN ASK, "TEACH US TO PRAY!"

This well-known children's mealtime prayer is an old-time favorite: "God is great, and God is good. Let us thank Him for our food. By His blessings, we are fed. Give us Lord, our daily bread. Amen." I think it is safe to say that every believer has, at one time or another, recited this prayer and taught their children to recite it as well. If you haven't, please do. It is very important to teach your children to pray, and the earlier the better. If you are not careful, however, this prayer—meant for good—may cause you to slack when you are trying to teach your children and grandchildren to effectively pray.

This is how you should teach this prayer:

"God is Great." Teach your children of God's greatness. *"Thine, O LORD, is the greatness, and the power, and the glory."* (1 Chronicles 29:11) Share a time when you experienced His greatness in your own life.

"God is Good." Teach them of God's goodness. When reciting the prayer, share with them a time that His goodness and mercy touched you or someone you know. *"For the LORD is Good: His mercy is everlasting."* (Psalm 100:5)

"Thank Him for this food." Teach them the importance of why we should give thanks. *"And Jesus took the loaves; and when He had given thanks, then he distributed the bread to His disciples."* (John 6:11) Share the story of how Jesus himself prayed over and blessed the meal. Then he gave the five loaves and two small fish to His disciples, and God miraculously used five small barley loaves and two fish to feed 5,000 people. Share this story with your children: five loaves, two fish, 5,000 people fed. Sounds like a miracle to me. Just saying!

"Give us LORD our daily bread." Teach your children that this prayer came from the Lord's Prayer in Luke 11:3: *"Give us day by day our daily bread."* Teach them that it is God who provides for their daily needs. Amen.

The disciples ask Jesus to teach them to pray.

> *And it came to pass, that, as he was praying in a certain place, when he ceased, one of his disciples said unto him, Lord, teach us to pray, as John also taught his disciples. And he said unto them, when you pray, say, Our Father which art in heaven, Hallowed be thy name. Thy kingdom come. Thy will be done, as in heaven, so in earth. Give us day by day our daily bread. And forgive us our sins; for we also forgive every one that is indebted to us. And lead us not into temptation; but deliver us from evil.* (Luke 11:1-4)

BEDTIME PRAYER

Another old-time favorite is the bedtime prayer: "Now I lay me down to sleep. I pray the Lord my soul to keep. If I should die before I wake, I pray to the lord my soul to take. Amen." I love this prayer because it speaks of peace, comfort, safety, surrender, death, and releasing ownership of your soul to God. This is a very powerful prayer for children and adults.

"Now I lay me done to sleep." You will find many Scriptures on sleep. I chose this one: *"In peace I will both lie down and sleep; for you alone, O LORD, make me dwell in safety."* (Psalm 4:8) Teach your children that God makes their dwelling place and their bedroom safe. As they close their eyes, they will know they are in a safe place.

"I pray the Lord my soul to keep." I think it is important for your children to have a clear understanding of what they are praying to assure them that God loves and promises to keep them. *"Nothing shall be able to separate us from the love of God, which is in Christ Jesus our Lord."* (Romans 8:39) This prayer teaches your children that they are safe in Christ Jesus.

"If I should die before I wake, I pray the Lord my soul to take." Here is a wonderful opportunity to share the plan of salvation with your children. *"For God so loved the world, that he gave His only Son, that whosoever believeth in him should not perish, but have everlasting life."* (John 3:16) I hope you will enjoy praying and sharing God's word with your children.

"O God, from my youth you have taught me, and I still proclaim your wondrous deeds." (Psalm 71:17)

YOU SHALL BE MY WITNESSES.

"But ye shall receive power, after the Holy Ghost is come upon you: and ye shall be witnesses unto me both in Jerusalem, and in all Judaea, and in Samaria, and unto the uttermost part of the earth." (Acts 1:8)

I have asked many born again believers if they have shared their salvation experience with family and friends. Most say "no," and their excuse is always the same. First, they say that they do not know how to witness. Second, they tell me that they do not know the Bible well enough to be a witness.

> When witnessing, start with the date and time, followed by the place.

I will address the first group. The definition of a "witness" is one who has personal knowledge of something or an event. My purpose here is to make witnessing simple for you and to remove your fears and anxieties. Think of a fun event you experience—perhaps a vacation. When you return, you share all the memories with your family and friends, down to the smallest of details. How fun and easy is that? When witnessing, start with the date and time, followed by the place. Was your experience of God's salvation at a church, home, or workplace? How did you hear the word? Was it from a friend, pastor, or religious program? Share these details and you will have shared your salvation experience!

For those of you who do not know the Scriptures, when witnessing, less Scripture is better. Sharing your *testimony* is more important to the lost person. They would much rather hear what God has done in your life than listen to you quote a bunch of Scripture.

Please write these three Scripture passages on an index card:

"For all have sinned and come short of the glory of God." (Romans 3:23)

Explain that all, including yourself, have sinned and need a Savior. Therefore, God sent his Son to die for us.

"For God so loved the world [YOU] that He gave His one and only Son, that whoever believes in Him shall not perish but have eternal life." (John 3:16) Explain that all God requires from us is to trust Him and believe that His Son Jesus died for you.

"If you declare with your mouth, Jesus is Lord and believe in your heart that God raised him from the dead, you will be saved." (Romans 10:9)

Then lead them in this prayer or use your own: "Father, I believe you sent your Son Jesus to die for my sins. I declare that He is my Lord and Savior, and I believe in my heart that You raised Him from the dead. I repent of my sins. Please forgive me and create in me a new heart. In Jesus' name, I pray." Amen.

Most likely, someone in your circle of friends needs to hear your testimony. Don't "SLACK!" They will thank you on judgment day.

"Likewise, I say unto you, there is joy in the presence of the angels of God over one sinner that repenteth." (Luke 15:10)

YOUR DREAMS & VISIONS:

_____
_____
_____
_____
_____
_____
_____
_____
_____
_____
_____
_____
_____
_____
_____
_____
_____
_____
_____
_____
_____
_____
_____
_____
_____
_____

6: AFAR OFF!

*"So, she went and came unto the man of God to Mount Carmel. And it came to pass, when the man of God saw her **afar off**, that he said to Gehazi his servant, 'Behold, yonder is that Shunammite.'"* (2 Kings 4:25)

In this passage, the Shunammite woman ran to Elisha, yet he saw her as being AFAR OFF. In this chapter, you will find that there are times when being close to God is not enough. You may still be afar off.

Let's get started.

This is another of God's promises: *"Draw nigh to God, and he will draw nigh to you."* (James 4:8) The Shunammite's journey to find Elisha is now complete, but she is still on a mission to see her son alive. For this to happen, she must stay focused and stay strong in faith. *"Run now, I pray thee, to meet her, and say unto her, Is it well with thee? Is it well with thy husband? Is it well with the child?" And she answered, "It is well."* (2 Kings 4:26) When Gehazi reached her, she turned her attention to him for just a moment to answer his questions.

WHEN TRAUMATIC EVENTS COME, DRAW NIGH TO GOD.

The hymn, "It Is Well with My Soul," was written by Horatio Spafford after three traumatic events in his life. The first two events were the death of his four-year-old son and the Great Chicago Fire of 1871, which ruined him financially. He had been a successful lawyer and had invested significantly in property around Chicago that was extensively damaged by the great fire. His business interests were further hit by the economic downturn of 1873. At that time, he planned a trip to England with his family on the *SS Ville du Havre* to help with D. L. Moody's upcoming evangelistic campaigns. In a late change of plans, he sent the family ahead, while he was delayed on business concerning zoning problems. While crossing the Atlantic Ocean, the ship sank rapidly after a collision with a sea vessel, the *Loch Earn*. All four of Spafford's daughters died. His wife Anna survived and sent him the now famous telegram, "Saved alone...." Shortly after, Spafford traveled to meet his grieving wife and was inspired to write these words as his ship passed near where his daughters had died:

When peace, like a river, attendeth my way,

When sorrows, like a sea billows roll; Whatever my lot, Thou, hast taught me to say, It is well, it is well with my soul.

Though Satan should buffet, though trials should come

Let this blest assurance control, that Christ has regarded my helpless estate

And has shed His own blood for my soul.

It is well with my soul.

Difficult events in your life will draw you closer to God and increase your faith. In these moments, God will give you the kind of faith that goes beyond "it is well": faith that goes beyond hope and faith that opens both the spiritual and physical eyes to the unseen promises and mysteries of God. Here, two parents—the Shunammite woman and Mr. Spafford—lost their children. Neither blamed God. Both trusted that He would keep his word. She believed that God would raise her son to live, and he believed that God had given his children eternal life through His Son, Jesus Christ. Both drew closer to God by standing on His promises.

Events such as these may strike at any moment, causing you to reject God, His love, and the promises you once believed.

My wife, Radena, and I were driving to Montgomery, Alabama to the Alpha Conference. We planned to attend the Caleb Connection—a requirement for all licensed and ordained ministers. We were driving north on Interstate 65 between Greenville and Montgomery, a stretch of highway that was under repair. For miles, all we saw were orange barrels and workers. As I drove, Radena read a book. I soon noticed a worker standing in a ditch and staring at the ground. He wore blue denim overalls and a white t-shirt. As soon as I saw him, God said to me: "Turn around and pray for him." I continued driving to the next exit, and as I veered onto the exit ramp, Radena ask why we were stopping. I said, "God asked me to stop and pray with one of the workers."

Driving back in the southbound lane, I looked across the median, trying to locate him. To my surprise, he had crossed over to the southbound lane and was standing next to the pavement. I pulled up right next to him. God is awesome! I walked to where he was standing and said, "I'm Pastor Leggett from

> Looking at me intently, he said, "Preacher, two weeks ago my granddaughter was struck by lightning, killing her.

Milton, Florida. My wife and I were driving to Montgomery, Alabama, when I saw you standing in the ditch staring at the ground. God told me to stop and pray for you." Looking at me intently, he said, "Preacher, two weeks ago my granddaughter was struck by lightning, killing her. I can't get over why this happened." He never said he was angry with God, nor did he blame God. He was searching for the answer as to why this happened to his grandbaby. I told him, "I do not have the answers as to why, but I do have God-assurance concerning your granddaughter. This comes to mind—Jesus said, 'Let the little children come to Me, and do not forbid them; for of such is the kingdom of heaven.' God loved your granddaughter. Paul wrote, 'We are confident, I say, and willing rather to be absent from the body and to be present with the Lord.'"

He then said, "Preacher, it's one thing for your family and friends to speak words of comfort in times of death, and we expect our pastor to do the same. But when a total stranger from another state pulls over to pray for me after God picked me out, this got my attention."

I answered: "The love God has for your granddaughter is the same love he has for you. He sent me to assure you that your granddaughter is in the presence of our Lord and Savior. She is no longer afar off." I finished with this Scripture: *"And if I go and prepare a place for you, I will come again, and receive you unto myself; that where I am, there ye may be also."* It was evident by the expression on his face that God had answered his "why." We prayed together, and he gave me a hug. Then I left for Montgomery. Over the years I have made many trips to Montgomery. Each time, I am reminded that you may find yourself in a ditch, but you are never alone.

THE COST OF SIN

"And David said unto Nathan, I have sinned against the LORD. And Nathan said unto David, The LORD also hath put away thy sin; thou shalt not die." (2 Samuel 12:13) In the Old and New Testaments, we see God's mercy, grace, and forgiveness.

While walking on his rooftop, King David noticed a beautiful woman bathing, so he asked his servant, "Who is this woman?" The servant told David that she was Uriah's wife, and her name was Bathsheba. Despite her marital status, David summoned her to the palace, and they slept together. They began having an affair, and she soon became pregnant with his child. To cover his sin, he had his friend Uriah killed. King David committed two grievous sins—against his friend and against his God. Let this be a warning to all of us: our eyes can cause us to lust over someone or something, resulting in our doing the unthinkable. Afterward, guilt and shame come, which make it difficult to worship. We find ourselves standing "Afar Off"

SIN WILL TAKE YOU FARTHER THAN YOU WANT TO GO, KEEP YOU LONGER THAN YOU WANT TO STAY, AND COST YOU MORE THAN YOU WANT TO PAY. —R. ZACHARIAS

So it is with you. Your sins give occasion for your enemies to separate you from God, family, and friends, by placing shame, guilt, and depression upon you. God will never do this to you! Before I tell you what God thinks about you and your sin, I must ask you something about yourself. Do you find it difficult to look into your wife's eyes, to look your friends and family in their eyes, or to lift your hands spiritually to God? If you answer "yes" to these questions, this is an indication that your enemy has placed shame, guilt, depression, or all three on you. How can you be sure? This Scripture should convince you: *"The thief cometh not, but to steal, and to kill and to destroy."* (John 10:10) He steals, kills, and destroys marriages; he steals, kills, and destroys friendships; he steals, kills, and destroys your relationship with your heavenly Father. This is what your enemy desires to do to you.

But your heavenly Father desires you: *"I am come that they might have life, and that they might have it more abundantly."* (John 10:10) By His grace, He came to give you abundant life in all areas of your life.

GOD GAVE DAVID ABUNDANT LIFE.

> *And Nathan departed unto his house. And the LORD struck the child that Uriah's wife bares unto David, and it was very sick. David therefore besought God for the child; and David fasted, and went in, and lay all night upon the earth. And the elders of his house arose, and went to him, to raise him up from the earth: but he would not, neither did he eat bread with them.* (2 Samuel 12:15-17)

Those who live secret lives think that they will never be caught or found out. King David was no different. He tried to conceal his affair. The more you try to cover your sins, the further you move away from God. I am sure you have heard that when you choose to lie, you must tell another lie to hold up the first, then another, again and again without end. This is a lesson for all of us. God did not accept David's fast nor will He accept yours when you lie to cover up your sin.

"For there is nothing covered, that shall not be revealed; neither hid, that shall not be known." (Luke 12:2)

> *And it came to pass on the seventh day, that the child died. And the servants of David feared to tell him that the child was dead: for they said, Behold, while the child was yet alive, we spake unto him, and he would not hearken unto our voice: how will he then vex himself, if we tell him that the child is dead? But when David saw that his servants whispered, David perceived that the child was dead: therefore, David said unto his servants, Is the child dead? And they said, He is dead.* (2 Samuel 12:18-19)

69

THE DEATH OF DAVID'S SON BRINGS TRUE REPENTANCE.

Then David arose from the earth, and washed, and anointed himself, and changed his apparel, and came into the house of the LORD, and worshipped: then he came to his own house; and when he required, they set bread before him, and he did eat. (2 Samuel 12:20)

There are seven things that David did after his son's death. First, he arose from the earth and his "guilt and shame." Then he washed himself—a normal reaction when you feel dirty from your sins and actions. You want to bathe. King David's sins had turned him into an evil man, doing the unthinkable. Be not deceived: sin will do the same to you.

Now, David realized that he is "Afar Off" from his God and must return to the House of the Lord. Washing with water was a ritual sign of holiness. The laws of Moses were commandments related to cleanliness and holiness, and washing with water was one of the primary ways that a person could be proclaimed "clean" or "sanctified." Today when we repent and return to God, He washes us from all unrighteousness.

"Come now, let us reason together, saith the Lord: though your sins be as scarlet, they shall be as white as snow; though they be red like crimson, they shall be as wool." (Isaiah 1:18)

David anointed himself, changed his clothes, and went to the house of the Lord to worship. Worship brings out many emotions—some of thanksgiving and others of sadness. The latter will make you seek God's forgiveness. Before David committed these sins, God said he was "a man after His own heart" (1 Samuel 13:14). Again, in the New Testament, David is described as a man after God's heart: *"And when he had removed him, he raised up unto them David to be their king; to whom also he gave their testimony, and said, 'I have found David the son of Jesse, a man after mine own heart, which shall fulfil all my will.'"* (Acts 13:22) David returned to God.

So, it is time for you to turn from your circumstances and seek God's forgiveness, grace, and love through your worship, letting Him know how grateful you are for giving you another chance to get things right. *"Seek ye the Lord while he may be found, call ye upon him while he is near: Let the wicked forsake his way, and the unrighteous man his thoughts: and let him return unto the Lord, and he will have mercy upon him; and to our God, for* **he will abundantly pardon."** (Isaiah 55:6-7)

The Shunammite woman ran to God for her miracle, it is time for you to run to God for yours.

HIS FIRST DISCIPLE, PETER

Read Luke 5:1-11.

Simon was on the shore with his brothers, cleaning his nets. Suddenly, a man appeared from out of the crowd and got into his boat. He asked Simon if he would push out a little from the shore. Then He sat down and taught the people from the boat. Simon soon learned that the man seated in his boat was like no one he had ever met.

> *When he had finished speaking, he said to Simon, "Put out into deep water, and let down the nets for a catch." And Simon answering said unto Him, "Master, we have toiled all the night and have taken nothing: nevertheless, at thy word I will let down the net."*
> (Luke 5:4-5)

Simon Peter was ready to go home, knowing the winds and tides were not right for him to continue fishing and thinking it would be a waste of time. Peter soon learned that whatever this man "Jesus" asked, he must trust Him and do, for He truly was the Son of God and Master of all.

> *When they had done so, they caught such many fish that their nets began to break. So they signaled their partners in the other boat to come and help them, and they came and filled both boats so full that they began to sink."* (Luke 5:6-7 NKJV)

THE IMPOSSIBLE CATCH

> *When Simon Peter saw this, he fell at Jesus' knees and said, 'Go away from me, Lord; I am a sinful man!' For he and all his companions were astonished at the catch of fish they had taken, and so were James and John, the sons of Zebedee, Simon's partners. Then Jesus said to*

Simon, 'Don't be afraid; from now on you will fish for people.' So they pulled their boats up on shore, left everything, and followed him. (Luke 5:8-11 NIV)

Jesus needed to do something extraordinary to get Peter's attention.

We have many firsts in our lives: first birthday, first day at school, first job, and, of course, first kiss. This was Peter's first miracle, but it was certainly not his last. Each miracle he experienced was designed by God to draw him spiritually closer and closer to his true purpose which was to build God's Kingdom—His Church. Simon Peter, a common guy that loved fishing, dreamed dreams and had visions of what he wanted in life, just like you and me. He worked hard, wanting to be successful, but the man who got into his boat changed everything. Peter planned his life, but in Jesus, he found new hope, directions, and dreams. Likewise, for us to turn and walk away from our dreams and plans, it would take something much higher than the plans and dreams we have. For Peter to walk away from what he had dedicated his entire life to, it had to be something for which he was willing to give up everything. Jesus needed to do something extraordinary to get Peter's attention. What better way than to beat him at something he was very good at: fishing?

PETER WALKS ON WATER.

"And Peter answered him and said, 'Lord, if it be thou, bid me come unto thee on the water.' And he said, 'Come.' And when Peter was come down out of the ship, he walked on the water, to go to Jesus." (Matthew 14:28-29)

Another first for Peter was walking on the water (a feat which has never been matched). Peter was a man of great faith, especially in the presence of his Lord and the other disciples. He was fearless. Some may even think of him as a risk taker, but he did not consider it a risk to totally trust in Jesus. You might be that person in your group who conquers the impossible, whatever it may be. Perhaps you always take the risk factor out and replace it with your confidence in Jesus. Do not worry if you make mistakes along the way. Be confident in this: God is more than able to fix all our mistakes.

Peter answered and said unto him, "Though all men shall be offended because of thee, yet will I never be offended." Jesus said unto him, "Verily I say unto thee, that this night, before the cock crows, thou shalt deny me thrice." (Matthew 26:33-34)

PETER DENIES JESUS FINDING HIMSELF AFAR OFF... WHY?

Now Peter sat without in the palace: and a damsel came unto him, saying, "Thou also wast with Jesus of Galilee." But he denied before them all, saying, "I know not what thou sayest." And when he was gone out into the porch, another maid saw him, and said unto them that were there, "This fellow was also with Jesus of Nazareth." And again, he denied with an oath, "I do not know the man." And after a while came unto him, they that stood by, and said to Peter, "Surely, thou also art one of them; for thy speech betrayeth thee." Then he began to curse and to swear, saying, "I know not the man." And immediately the cock crew. And Peter remembered the word of Jesus, which said unto him, "Before the cock crows, thou shalt deny me thrice." And he went out and wept bitterly. (Matthew 26:69-75)

When Peter heard the cock crow, he wept. What happened to make him renounce his Lord? Peter witnessed the miracle of his nets filling with fish, nearly sinking his ship. He walked on water with Jesus. Jesus healed his mother-in-law. Then, Peter witnessed and caused Jesus' last recorded miracle. Peter drew his sword, smote the high priest's servant, and cut off his right ear. Then Jesus touched the servant's ear and healed him. He spent years with Jesus, listening to Him as He taught His word to the people. He was with Jesus in the upper room. So, what happened?

Here is the reason that Peter renounced his Lord: for the first time in three years, he found himself alone. Peter witnessed the Lord being arrested, and Jesus was taken from him. On top of that, all the disciples were scattered and in hiding. Please hear me! It is dangerous for you to stop attending church or to stop hanging out with your Christian friends. You have heard it said that there is strength in numbers. We know this is true. God says, *"Not forsaking the assembling of ourselves together, as the manner of some is; but exhorting one another: and so much the more, as ye see the day approaching."* (Hebrews 10:25) We must stay connected.

> Miracles do not produce faith. It is faith that produces miracles.

All the people Peter loved and trusted were "afar off." Finding himself alone and feeling trapped by the angry mob who sought to kill his Lord, he let fear rob him of the memory of the miracles he witnessed. His faith was crushed. This I know, miracles do not produce faith. It is faith that produces miracles. Stop chasing miracles and start chasing your God-given measure of faith. There will come a time when your memory of past miracles will not carry you through the valley of fear. It is your faith in God that will take you across the valley to the other side.

Someone told me a story. A teenage boy lived with his parents in a logging town. While on summer vacation, he got a job working in a logging camp. His father thought it was wonderful, but his mother was unsure. She did not want her boy staying over the summer with the rough men who worked in the camp. She had heard what kind of things went on at the camp. She feared the men would give him a hard time when they learned he was a Christian.

When summer vacation ended, everyone was excited to have him home. His mother asked him how things went at the camp and how the men reacted when they discovered he was a Christian. The son said everything went fine and that they treated him like one of the guys because he never told them he was a Christian. Does this remind you of someone you know? Did you hear the cock crow? The young man's own actions placed him "afar off."

"For whosoever shall be ashamed of me and of my words, of him shall the Son of man be ashamed, when he shall come in his own glory, and in his Father's, and of the holy angels." (Luke 9:26)

YOUR DENIAL

You invite your friends over for a cookout and pool party. When doing some last-minute cleaning, you notice you left your Bible on the coffee table, so you put it in a drawer out of sight. Do you hear the rooster crow? At work, coworkers tell a racial joke. You laugh with them. Do you hear the rooster crow? You turn on the car radio to your favorite station which is blaring profanity and words that degrade women. Do you hear the rooster crow? What are you doing that makes the rooster crow? What causes you to be "afar off"?

Are you ashamed of Jesus? What has He done to embarrass you? Does the fact He is the Son of God embarrass you? Yea, I can see that. Who in the world would want to be seen hanging out with God's Son? Think about this: not one of your sins embarrassed Jesus—your lies—your stealing—adultery—murder—you fill in the blanks. Jesus died to forgive you of all your sins because He loves you, so why are you embarrassed by Him. I think I know the answer: *"These people draweth nigh unto me with their mouth, and honoureth me with their lips; but their heart is far from me."* (Matthew 15:8) Your heart is "afar off."

You still have time to get things right. Start by honoring Jesus with your heart. Take the Bible out of the drawer and leave it on the coffee table. Stop listening to racial jokes. Tell your friends that God created everyone in His image and likeness. Change your radio channel to one that honors Jesus. When Jesus comes in all His glory, He will not be ashamed of you.

"Jesus saith unto him, I am the way, the truth, and the life: No man cometh unto the Father, but by me." (John 14:6)

"DRAW NIGH."

NOTES:

_____

_____

_____

_____

_____

_____

_____

_____

_____

_____

_____

_____

_____

_____

_____

_____

_____

_____

_____

_____

_____

_____

_____

_____

_____

_____

_____

_____

_____

7: LET HER ALONE

*And when she came to the man of God to the hill, she caught him by the feet: but Gehazi came near to thrust her away. And the man of God said, **'Let her alone';** for her soul is vexed within her: and the Lord hath hid it from me, and hath not told me.* (2 Kings 4:27)

"Then she said, 'Did I desire a son of my lord? Did I not say, do not deceive me?'" (2 Kings 4:28)

After running for hours, the Shunammite woman finally reached the man of God. She embraced Him by his feet. Gehazi came to thrust her away, and Elisha said, "Let her alone." In other words, he said, "Do not harm her." *"God is a shield unto them that put their trust in Him."* (Psalm 31:32) Here, God speaks through His prophet, commanding His servant to leave her alone. God protects His daughter as He would you. He knew Elisha needed no protection from her. Elisha was not in any danger, so why did Gehazi see her as a threat?

This is what I think happened, causing Gehazi to react the way he did. While searching for Elisha, the Shunammite woman overcame many obstacles. There was one final obstacle standing between her and the prophet: her friend Gehazi. After taking time to answer Gehazi's questions, she stepped past him. Feeling the adrenaline and her emotions rushing through her body, her eyes fixed on Elisha, the man of God. She began to run. Not slowing to kneel, she dove at his feet. All of this happened so quickly that the reaction of the servant was first and foremost to protect his lord. However, the Shunammite woman's mind was made up. Nothing would separate her and Elisha until he agreed to return to Shunem with her.

> *For I am persuaded, that neither death, nor life, nor angels, nor principalities, nor powers, nor things present, nor things to come, nor height, nor depth, nor any other creature, shall be able to separate us from the love of God, which is in Christ Jesus our Lord.* (Romans 8:38)

Paul is persuaded, and so am I, that none of these events in our life will separate us from God.

1. Death will not separate us.

Death. This is a topic that most people avoid discussing. The Bible says, *"It is appointed unto men once to die...."* (Hebrews 9:27) I believe that fear of the unknown causes us to shy away from conversations regarding death. Death seems so final, but is it? In the Bible, we find that death is not the end of our existence. It is God's plan to bring us into His eternal presence and give us eternal life.

The Shunammite woman knew that the death of her son was not final. She was confident that her son would live again. But Lazarus's sisters were not so confident regarding their brother. He had two sisters, Martha and Mary. They sent word to Jesus that their brother Lazarus was sick. When Jesus received their message, He knew that the sickness was not unto death, so He stayed two more days. Afterwards, he told the disciples, "Our friend Lazarus sleeps, I will go to wake him." His disciples said, "If he sleeps, he shall do well." Then Jesus plainly said, "Lazarus is dead."

When Martha heard that Jesus was coming, she went out to meet Him, saying, "If you had been here, my brother would not have died. But even now I know whatever you ask of God, He will do." Jesus said to her, "Your brother will rise again for I am the resurrection and the life." Then He went to Lazarus's grave. He cried with a loud voice, "Lazarus, come forth." Lazarus came out of the tomb, bound hand

and foot with graveclothes. Jesus said, "loose him," to those who were there, and they let him go.

"O death, where is thy sting? O grave, where is thy victory? The sting of death is sin, and the strength of sin is the law. But thanks be to God, which giveth us the victory through our Lord Jesus Christ."
(1 Corinthians 15:55-57)

2. Life will not separate us from God's love.

If you ask me to explain life, I will use Joel 3:14: *"Multitudes, multitudes, in the valley of decisions! For the day of the Lord is near in the valley of decisions."* **Life is a *valley of decisions*.** From the moment your alarm clock wakes you, you start planning your day. But your enemy satan will attempt to turn your good intentions into temptations, for he is very aware that temptations will separate you from God. He himself was cast out of heaven due to his "pride" which caused him to rebel against God. Satan was tempted to take from God the praise and glory reserved only for God. Let's face it, we are tempted every day, and each temptation is designed to separate us from God and His love.

The good news is that satan cannot force you to do anything. You no longer have the excuse, "The devil made me do it." God has given you a way to escape every temptation known to man. Instead of caving into satan's devices, look for the way out. God never says that He will remove the temptation. He promises to walk with you through them, making sure you have a way to escape each one as He did for the Shunammite woman. Life, with all its decisions and temptations, cannot separate you from God.

There hath no temptation taken you, but such as is common to man: but God is faithful, who will not suffer you to be tempted above that ye are able; but will with the temptation also make a way to escape, that ye may be able to bear it. (1 Corinthians 10:13)

Now satan knows he cannot separate you from God and His love, so his next tactic is to keep you apart physically and mentally. He knows that your friends can influence you to stay apart. You raised your children to know the importance of serving God by attending church, but your son is now at an age where he can play little league baseball and your daughter can be a cheerleader for the team. While at your friend's cookout, you notice his son wearing his new little league uniform. Your friend says, "Man, I could really use your boy on the team. I know you attend church, but this league is only nine weeks. We play Sunday mornings." Your son hears the conversation and says, "Dad, can I play, please?" You and his mother decide to let him play and your daughter is a cheerleader for his team. For the next nine Sundays, your family is at the ballfield. During those same weeks, your supervisor calls you to his office and says, "We are behind on production. I need everyone to work 12-hour shifts for the next three months."

So now you are missing Sunday mornings and Wednesday night services. Like I said, satan cannot separate you from God, but he can keep you apart if you let him. Do you find this to be true in your life? *"For what shall it profit a man, if he shall gain the whole world, and lose his own soul? Or what shall a man give in exchange for his soul?"* (Mark 8:36-37)

Where can I go from Your Spirit? Or where can I flee from Your presence? If I ascend into heaven, you are there; If I make my bed in hell, behold, You are there. If I take the wings of the morning, and dwell in the uttermost parts of the sea, even there Your hand shall lead me, and Your right hand shall hold me. (Psalm 139:7-10 NKJV)

If you climb to the top of Mount Everest, God is with you, or find yourself in the deepest part of the ocean, He is with you. Neither height nor depth can separate you from God.

Now, are you convinced that nothing can separate you from God and His love? I say to those who are running to God, keep running. To you, who are searching God's word, keep searching. If you are singing, keep on singing. To you, called to preach, keep preaching. To you, dancing before the Lord, keep dancing. *"Wearing a linen ephod, David was dancing before the Lord with all his might."* (2 Samuel 6:14) Whatever you are doing for God, do it with all you might. But a warning to you who hinder those who are, God says: "LET THEM ALONE."

As we continue reading verse 27, we see Elisha's observation regarding the Shunammite woman: *"for her soul is vexed within her: and the Lord hath not told me."* (2 Kings 4:27) This mother's heart and soul were vexed. From the moment her son died in her arms, she knew that his death was not final. This is the reason she kept her son's condition secret.

She decreed that her son would live again in the secret place of her heart. There are things hidden in your heart from everyone but God. God did not tell Elisha that her son was dead because God is the Alpha and the Omega—the beginning and the end. He knew her son would live again.

WHAT YOU DECREE SHALL BE ESTABLISHED.

"But thou, when thou prayest, enter thy closet, and when thou hast shut thy door, pray to thy Father which is in secret; and thy Father which seeth in secret shall reward thee openly." (Matthew 6:6)

A "decree" is an official order issued by a legal authority (YOU). In her heart, the Shunammite woman had decreed that she would soon embrace her son again. He "Who seeth in secret" shall reward you openly, if you continue in the faith. We know

> Why are some prayers answered and some are not? It comes down to the attitude of the person praying.

this to be true, so why are some prayers answered and some are not? It comes down to the attitude of the person praying. Many smaller churches start their mid-week services with testimonies meant to celebrate God's goodness in their lives, but some use these services to draw attention and sympathy to themselves: "Oh, the devil has worked me over this week; I need your prayers."

"Thou shalt also decree a thing, and it shall be established unto thee: and the light shall shine upon thy ways." (Job 22:28)

What you decree shall be established. Even if you had a trying week, you must always give God praise in everything. Say it this way, "I give praise to Jesus Christ my Lord for this week. He walked with me every step of the way. Despite what the devil meant for my evil; God used for my good. He made me more than a conqueror." What you prayed for in your closet should stay in the closet and not be used in the mid-week service to have people feel sorry for you. God was with you in your prayer closet but may not have answered your prayer because of the words of doubt you used during the midweek service or while on the phone to a friend when you said, "Oh pitiful me," giving honoring to satan and not God. It's time you ask in faith, not doubting!

"But let him ask in faith, nothing wavering. For he that waveth is like a wave of the sea driven with the wind and tossed. For let not that man think that he shall receive anything of the Lord." (James 1:6-7)

When God spoke the words, "Let her alone," through His prophet, it was not the last time He used a prophet, preacher, priest, or you to speak words of warning. Today, He continues to warn those who are messing with His children. If you are that person, take heed to His warning. Here is a Scripture passage that you most likely have heard or used to encourage a friend under attack: *"No weapon that is formed against thee shall prosper."* (Isaiah 54:17) Many people have found comfort in these words at one time or another.

You may know people who have been hurt by words spoken over them. If we are not diligent when using the written word of God, satan will cause us to leave out the fullness of a passage of Scripture. Here is a perfect example: the verse I referenced contains a second part which most people leave out. *"And every tongue that shall rise up against thee in judgement thou shall condemn. This is the heritage of the servants of the Lord, and their righteousness is of me, saith the Lord."* This part explains why the weapons cannot prosper. It speaks of our heritage and our righteousness.

1. **Heritage:** Your Godly heritage cannot be displayed as your worldly accomplishments are, nor numbered by trophies, metals, or certificates hanging in your office. Your heritage is a covenant between God and his children and is without end. It cannot be measured, for it is spiritual, eternal, and passes from generation to generation. So, how do you display your heritage? Your actions speak louder than trophies, certificates, or words. Do your actions display your heritage? When your family and friends hear you speak Godly words and your actions reflect the same, you are passing your heritage to all who know you and hear you.

2. **Righteousness:** You cannot earn your righteousness nor your salvation by good works or by keeping the law. *"For ALL have sinned and come short of the glory of God,"* but many will try, only to be disappointed time and again by their failures. So, what does God think about your righteousness?

All your righteousness is as a filthy rag (Isaiah 64:6). It stinks to God like your dirty laundry left in the clothes hamper and found months later. What must you do to earn righteousness? You can't, for it is God's gift to believers. *"Even the righteousness of God which is by faith of Jesus Christ unto all and upon all of them that believe: for there is no difference."* (Romans 3:22) If you are a believer, you are covered by God's righteousness. The robe of his righteousness is given to you.

Righteousness is attained by faith, not by works. By faith, we are accounted as righteous. Abraham was accounted as righteous not because of what he did, but because of his faith in God. If by works we are accounted righteous, God would have accounted Abraham righteous by his works, but this is not so. Your robe of righteousness is only attainable by your faith in God.

The Apostle Paul confirms this by saying that works are counted as a debt, not grace. Justification **by faith**: *"For by grace you have been **saved** through **faith;** and that not of yourselves, it is the gift of God; not as a result of **works,** so that no one may boast."* (Ephesians 2:8-9) A Christian is **saved** by grace and by grace only—not because of **works**.

For you to be clothed with Jesus Christ's robe of righteousness, you do not need works, only faith: *"the righteousness of God which is by faith of Jesus Christ."* (Romans 3:22)

The Shunammite woman knew how to tap into her heritage, and so she did on several occasions, claiming what was rightfully hers by her assurance as a daughter of God. I love this passage where we see once again how God sends out a warning to everyone who speaks words against His children. Part of your heritage is that you do not have to prove yourself against false accusers. God does this for you. God says that our righteousness is of Him. Stop trying to prove to people that you are righteous. Your proof is telling others that God sent His only Son to die for you, and through Him, you are made righteous.

"I will greatly rejoice in the Lord, my soul shall be joyful in my God; for he hath clothed me with **the garments of salvation,** he hath covered me with **the robe of righteousness,** as a bridegroom decketh himself with ornaments, and as a bride adorneth herself with her jewels."* (Isaiah 61:10)

"THEIR SINS, I REMEMBER NO MORE" (HEBREWS 10:17).

"Lord I have made a mess of my life and I need your help."

In November 1985, while I was a patient at the Pavilion, a drug rehab center at West Florida Hospital, I rededicated my life to Jesus. The first day of a 29-day treatment program, I was asked to participate in prayers. I told them I was not there to pray. I just wanted to complete the program to save my job. I did not tell them that I had no intention of quitting my drinking and drugs. However, hearing them pray for the next 14 days pricked my heart, and I changed my mind. I remember going to my room, getting down on my knees, and looking out the window while I prayed this simple prayer: "Lord I have made a mess of my life and I need your help." At that very moment, He delivered me from my addictions and forgave my sins.

I recall looking at my hands. I knew God had done something, but I was not sure what. The next morning as I got in line for my meds, I told Mary our nurse that I no longer needed to take the meds. Thinking that I was trying to cause trouble, she said, "Mr. Leggett, you have to take your meds." I reminded her how my hands shook yesterday and told her that the night before, I had prayed in my room and instantly the shakes stopped. The doctor heard our conversation and asked what my problem was, for he had witnessed my prior behavior. I truly was a problem child. I said, "There's no problem doc. You saw my hands yesterday. Look at them now. After I prayed last night, they stopped shaking."

He told me to go exercise with the other clients, and afterward he would check my vitals. While checking my blood pressure, he slowly turned his head from the cup on my arm. Looking at me, he said, "I don't understand. It's normal." I told him that after I prayed, God took away the shakes. From that day, he removed me from all medication. I called my wife and asked her to bring me a Bible. After receiving it, I started witnessing. All but one rejected God's word. A man named Joe prayed to receive Jesus as his Lord and Savior. After completing the program, I stayed in contact with the doctor and nursing staff. Two years later, my nurse Mary called and said that the doctor wanted to see me. During my conversation with him, he asked, "When you were here, you took a more spiritual route than the program itself offers." When I affirmed that this was true, he asked if I would come back to teach a class on the spiritual aspects of recovery. Of course, with a big smile on my face, I said "yes."

Five years after God healed and delivered me, I met with our church board for a position as lead pastor. I will never forget the conversation I had with God as I drove to the church. He said to tell them everything about my past and to hide nothing. I thought that if I did, they would never vote me in as their pastor. Then He said, if you tell them everything, satan will have nothing to use against you. After the meeting, they asked me to step outside while they voted. Before leaving the room, I said, "I must tell you more about my past, things you did not ask me." Then, I told them everything. I left the room, thinking they would never vote me in, but they did…100%.

Years later, a visiting preacher noticed how our church membership had grown and decided that he wanted to be lead pastor. He privately met with the church board to tell them about my past. To his surprise, the board said, "Our pastor has already told us about those things." God defeated satan years earlier when He told me to tell the church board everything. Don't hide from your past. Let God cover it with His blood. I served as lead pastor for seven years.

SATAN'S DESIRE IS TO KEEP YOU IN DARKNESS.

"And they came to Jericho: and as he went out of Jericho with his disciples and a great number of people, blind Bartimaeus, the son of Timaeus, sat by the highway side begging." (Mark 10:46)

Bartimaeus heard the shuffling of sandals and people talking excitedly around him. He was a homeless person, reaching for his clay cup and holding it in the direction of the noise. He was trapped in total darkness by his blindness and started doing the only thing he knew, and that was to beg. Bartimaeus was about to meet travelers who were not like the others. In the group passing by, he would encounter the One who had the power to give sight to the blind.

"And when he heard it was Jesus of Nazareth, he began to cry out, and say, thou son of David have mercy on me." (Mark 10:47)

He changed his cry from begging for money and food, to pleading for mercy. Those walking with Jesus told him to hold his peace—in other words, to keep his mouth shut. Fearing his blindness and thinking this might be his only chance to meet Jesus, he cried out even louder. Hearing the cries of Bartimaeus, Jesus stood still, then commanded that Bartimaeus be brought to Him. Here's another example of God standing for his children saying to His disciples "Let him alone". They called out to the blind man, saying, "Jesus is calling for you." He immediately rose and cast away his garment. Jesus said to him, "What would you have me do?" He said, "That I may receive my sight." Jesus said to him, "Go thy way." Perhaps Bartimaeus thought that Jesus did absolutely nothing for him.

Bartimaeus—still in total darkness—must have thought: "Why would Jesus send me away?" After hearing Jesus' words, the seconds that passed must have seemed like an eternity. Then he heard Jesus speak again, and what He said changed his life forever. Jesus said, "Bartimaeus, your faith has made you whole." Immediately, he received his sight. Jesus convinced Bartimaeus that if he continued to beg, he would never receive his sight. This is a lesson for you as well. Jesus is asking, "What would you have me do? Ask and you shall receive."

> Stop begging. This very act separates you from God, and makes you feel unworthy, like an outsider and not God's child.

So, stop begging. This very act separates you from God, and makes you feel unworthy, like an outsider and not God's child. You will never hear your heavenly Father say to you: "If you want anything from me, you must beg for it." The act of begging separated the lepers from friends, family, and God until one had the faith to step out from the multitude and say, "Lord, if thou will, thou canst make me clean." Jesus touched him, saying, "I will; be thou clean," and immediately his leprosy was cleansed. The Shunammite woman never begged. She asked God for the things she needed.

The entire time, Bartimaeus and the leper had all the power they needed—their faith—but they did not know how to use it. Jesus made it very clear that, by faith, Bartimaeus would receive his sight and the leper would be cleansed, but only after asking to receive sight and be healed from leprosy.

"For everyone that asketh receiveth; and he that seeketh findeth; and to him that knocketh it shall be opened." (Matthew 7:8)

WHEN YOU ASK—YOU SHALL RECEIVE.

NOTES:

_____

_____

_____

_____

_____

_____

_____

_____

_____

_____

_____

_____

_____

_____

_____

_____

_____

_____

_____

_____

_____

_____

_____

_____

_____

_____

8: GIRD UP THY LOINS

"Then he said to Gehazi, 'Gird up thy loins, and take my staff in thine hand, and go thy way. If thou meet any man, salute him not; and if any salute thee, answer him not again; and lay my staff upon the face of the child.'"
(2 Kings 4:29)

GIRD UP THY LOINS

You can tell by the instructions Elisha gave Gehazi that there's a sense of urgency: "If you meet any man, salute him not." My mother would have said "Don't lollygag around." The journey back to her son is beginning in the same way as the woman's journey to find the prophet. The servant does not have time to greet those he may meet along the way.

Elisha's first instruction was for the servant to "gird up his loins," meaning to prepare and strengthen himself for what was to come physically, mentally, and spiritually. He was to get ready for hard work and difficult circumstances during the return trip to Shunem. Now you have the meaning of the word "gird": to prepare oneself for action.

The Shunammite woman must soon return to her son, and she must stay focused, not allowing distractions to cause her to fear and doubt, for both would weaken her faith. As believers, we are encouraged to gird up the loins of our mind—be prepared for action. In doing so, we keep a sober and alert spirit.

> *Wherefore gird up the loins of your mind, be sober, and hope to the end for the grace that is to be brought unto you at the revelation of Jesus Christ; as obedient children, not fashioning yourselves according to the former lusts in your ignorance: but as he which hath called you is holy, so be ye holy in all manner of conversation; because it is written, "Be ye holy; for I am holy."*
> (1 Peter 1:13-16)

God tells us in Scripture: *"For they that are after the flesh do mind the things of the flesh; but they that are after the Spirit the things of the Spirit. For to be carnally minded is death; but to be spiritually minded is life and peace."* (Romans 8:5-6)

PREPARING FOR HER SON'S MIRACLE

> Those distractions from within are the ones that quickly destroy faith, hope, and belief.

As she moves closer to receiving her son's miracle, she experiences more distractions. Most come from without, and these are much easier to overcome. On the other hand, those distractions from within are the ones that quickly destroy faith, hope, and belief. These are often memories of past events. You have both carnal and spiritual minds, and you must control both. What impressed me about the Shunammite mother is that she took control of her minds and her destiny. She was not timid when it came to telling the man of God that she desired for him to return with her to Shunem.

"If ye abide in me, and my words abide in you, ye shall ask what ye will, and it shall be done unto you." (John 15:7)

Her return trip would be more challenging than her trip to find Elisha, because finding the man of God was not a miracle. She used her carnal mind, but now the challenges she faced were totally different. To receive her son's miracle, she had to stay spiritually minded, wiping out every carnal thought that brought death and not life. To do this, she had to stay close ("nigh") to Elisha. As Elisha vowed to stay with Elijah to receive his miracle of the double portion, she must stay close to Elisha to receive her son's miracle. In the same way, we are told to *"draw nigh to God, and He will draw nigh to you."* (James 4:8)

We are often guilty of quoting only the part of a verse that makes us feel good. Here is a perfect example: "Draw nigh to God and he will draw nigh to you." How many times have you told a friend or family member to "draw nigh to God"? Saying or praying these words alone will not move God. This verse has a condition: do everything that God instructs you to do.

Submit yourselves therefore to God. Resist the devil, and he will flee from you. Draw nigh to God, and he will draw nigh to you. Cleanse your hands, ye sinners; and purify your hearts, ye double minded. Be afflicted, and mourn, and weep: let your laughter be turned to mourning, and your joy to heaviness. Humble yourselves in the sight of the Lord, and he shall lift you up. (James 4:7-10)

1. Submit yourselves to God.

The very act of drawing close to God starts by totally submitting yourself to Him. The Shunammite woman gives a perfect example of submitting to God. As you recall in the previous chapters, when she realized he was a holy man of God, she submitted to his authority. So too, we must submit to God's authority. In doing so, we find liberty. His Holy Spirit gives us directions. To submit means to yield oneself to the power or authority of another. *"No man can serve two masters: for either he will hate the one and love the other; or else he will hold to the one and despise the other. Ye cannot serve God and mammon."* (Matthew 6:24)

2. Resist the devil.

God promises that if you resist the devil, he will flee from you. How long will you continue to give the devil permission to hang out in your mind? Start resisting him and his lies. If you are not resisting the devil, do not expect God to draw nigh to you. Don't kid yourself. If you're not drawing nigh to God, you're going the other way.

"Submit yourselves therefore to God. Resist the devil, and he will flee from you." (James 4:7)

3. Cleanse your hands.

God is calling us to live holy lives and to stop sinning. He is concerned about our worldly activities and sinful deeds. God issues a similar warning through His prophet Isaiah: *"Wash you, make you clean; put away the evil of your doings from before mine eyes; cease to do evil."* (Isaiah 1:16) In this verse, God reminds us of our fallen state. We are sinners. We must forever be mindful of this fact, that our salvation is a gift from God, and only by His grace are we saved. We should always show our gratitude to God by our actions.

4. Purify your hearts.

The best way to purify your heart is spending time in prayer and studying God's word. Both will remove the cares of this world and replace them with spiritual thoughts. As you can see, God clearly connects your mind, your emotions, and your will, to the heart. What does God think about your heart?

"Set your affections on things above, not on things of the earth." (Colossians 3:2) The Shunammite woman's actions are clear. Her affections and cares are on things above and not of this world.

5. Double-minded.

Are you a double-minded person? If so, you need to know God's thoughts about those who are double-minded, but first, let's look at the definition.

"A double-minded person is restless and confused in his thoughts, his actions, and his behavior. Such a person is always in conflict with himself. One torn by such inner conflict can never lean with confidence on God and His gracious promises" *(Got Questions)*.

"I know thy works, that thou art neither cold nor hot: I would thou wert cold or hot. So then because thou art lukewarm, and neither cold nor hot, I will spew thee out of my mouth." (Revelation 3:15-16)

6. Humble yourselves.

"If my people, which are called by my name, shall humble themselves, and pray, and seek my face, and turn from their wicked ways; then will I hear from heaven, and will forgive their sin, and will heal their land." (2 Chronicles 7:14)

Let's make this scripture personal. "If I, which are called by His name, shall humble myself, and pray, and seek His face and turn from my wicked ways; then will God hear from heaven, and will forgive my sin, and will heal my land."

Now you can draw nigh to God, and He will draw nigh to you.

In the presence of the man of God, the Shunammite woman has her mind on God alone. Elisha represents the One she trusts—God Himself. She is now only a few hours from her son's miracle. How exciting it would be, knowing you were only a few hours from receiving a miracle in your own life. You can experience miracles like the Shunammite woman by setting your affections and cares on the things above and forgetting the cares of this world which bring death.

CARNAL MIND

One Sunday morning, during our altar service at Munson Assembly of God Church, Mr. Evers—a member on our worship team—requested prayer for his brother. After praying over his request, I felt a need to take a prayer cloth from the altar, anoint it with oil, and put it in my wallet. That morning as I was leaving the church, Mr. Evers stopped me in the parking lot. He asked if I would go to the hospital to pray with his brother. "Of course," I said, even after he told me that his brother despised preachers and that he may not receive me or let me pray for him.

The next day I visited his brother. Entering his room, I introduced myself. He immediately took control of the conversation. The Lord told me to hold my peace and let him do the talking. I did, and he told me stories of his childhood and his service in the military. This went on for about thirty minutes until I heard the Spirit say, "Tell him why you came today." I began to tell him why I was there, but again he took over the conversation, saying, "I know you came to pray and lay hands on me, but if you try, I will rip your arm off." The countenance on his face changed, and I saw the anger in his eyes.

I tried to explain that I was there at the request of his brother, but he would have none of that. When he told me that I should leave, I turned to his wife and could see she was embarrassed. Not sure what to do next, I stood still, waiting for God's directions. God reminded me of the prayer cloth in my wallet. Now, I knew what to do. I agreed with Mr. Evers and said, "Before I go, I would like to leave a prayer cloth with you. I will not touch you; I will give it to your wife." After several minutes, he finally said, "Okay. You can leave the prayer cloth."

As soon as it touched him, he began to cry.

I asked his wife if she had a safety pin that she could use to pin the prayer cloth to his hospital gown. Looking through her purse, she realized she had no pin, but she found a band-aid. I said that would work fine and told her to tape it near the top of his gown. She did as I said, and as soon as it touched him, he began to cry. Now I knew why God had me anoint the prayer cloth. He knew that Mr. Evers would not let me lay hands on him nor pray for him. The cloth represented my prayers and faith in God for him. As he continued crying, he said, "I have people who love me." I said, "Yes you do, and Jesus loves you more than all your friends and family together." With tears on his cheeks, he said, "He loves me, doesn't he?"

That morning, he repented and asked Jesus into his heart. With tears of joy, his wife gave me a hug. Before I left, he asked if I would visit him again. I said, "Of course," and visited him often for the next several weeks. During my last visit, before he was released, I invited them to church on Sunday. He wanted to go but felt it would be best to stay home and rest. I said, "What if we do this? I will have our ladies in the church prepare lunch after the morning service. We will come to your home with our worship team and have fellowship with you and your wife." He agreed, and that's what we did.

As the day approached, his brother told me that for years they'd had a strained relationship and that he'd better not go. I reminded him that he had asked me to go to the hospital, and now, I was asking him to bring his guitar and meet us at his brother's home. Ultimately, he agreed, adding that he couldn't believe his brother was allowing a preacher into his home. I will never forget that Sunday. The lunch was awesome. Our praise team led us in worship, and I gave a short devotion. That morning, God healed the brothers' relationship and restored the love and joy in Mr. and Mrs. Evers' marriage.

SET YOUR AFFECTIONS ON THINGS ABOVE.

For years, Mr. Evers' affections were on the things of this world. To be carnally minded brings death. As our friendship grew, I asked him what caused him to have such disdain for preachers. He said, "I'm embarrassed to tell you. When I was a young man, I purchased a hog from a preacher. When I gave him the money, he could not make change. I said, 'That's alright. You can give it to me later.' He never did. So, over a few dollars, I grew bitter, and I was convinced that all preachers were liars. Satan used this to rob me of years of joy, until you came."

That Sunday morning, God removed the bitterness and unforgiveness from his heart. *"Let all bitterness and wrath and anger and clamor and slander be put away from you, along with all malice."* (Ephesians 4:31)

In an instant, God destroyed Satan's deception, which he held over Mr. Evers for years. God restored to him the years of stolen joy, and he received the peace that passes all understanding. *"I will restore to you the years that the swarming locust has eaten."* (Joel 2:25) God will restore to you everything that has been lost and broken.

You must set your affection on the things above, because being spiritually minded brings life and peace. I ask you, why let circumstances cause you to grow bitter? You should never believe the lies of the enemy. Instead, stand tall and tell the world with confidence: "My Lord will restore me. Jesus is more than qualified." He conquered the cross and the tomb for you, so you can enjoy His incomparable restoration.

What I learned about the Shunammite woman is that she is driven by the words from God's prophet. We shall see how her faith in God guided her as she made the right choices concerning her son. Are you making the right choices? What has God told you to "gird up" in your personal life?

Your loins? Your mind? Could it be something that only you and God know—an area of weakness where you struggle? You're not alone. We all have times when we fall short and need help, and that's okay if you are man or woman enough to admit it and ask God for help.

"For all have sinned and come short of the glory of God." (Romans 3:23)

Do you remember a time when someone shared this verse with you? Perhaps you read it yourself and God said, "Gird up your mind and heart with the truth of these words." Accepting the truth, you repented and received forgiveness and new birth. Wanting to please your family and God, you promised them to always do the right thing, but you slipped up. My friend, you are not the first and you certainly are not the last who failed God after receiving His forgiveness. Let me assure you that God didn't use up all his forgiveness on you the day you repented. However, you must learn from your mistakes.

The apostle Paul revealed his weakness as he struggled to do the right thing:

> *For I know that in me (that is, in my flesh) dwelleth no good thing: for to will is present with me; but how to perform that which is good I find not. For the good that I would I do not: but the evil which I would not, that I do.* (Romans 7:18-19)

> *What shall we say then? Shall we continue in sin, that grace may abound? God forbid. How shall we, that are dead to sin, live any longer therein? Know ye not, that so many of us as were baptized into Jesus Christ were baptized into his death? Therefore, we are buried with him by baptism into death: that like as Christ was raised up from the dead by the glory of the Father, even so we also should walk in newness of life.* (Romans 6:1-4)

Ask God to reveal the areas in your personal life that need repair; then spiritually gird each one in your mind and heart as you ask God to give you the wisdom and knowledge to restore life to each one.

"GIRD UP YOUR HEART AND MIND WITH THE HOLY SPIRIT."

NOTES:

_____

_____

_____

_____

_____

_____

_____

_____

_____

_____

_____

_____

_____

_____

_____

_____

_____

_____

_____

_____

_____

_____

_____

_____

_____

_____

9: TAKE MY STAFF

*Then he said to Gehazi, "Gird up thy loins, **and take my staff in thine hand,** and go thy way: if thou meet any man, salute him not; and if any salute thee, answer him not again: and lay my staff upon the face of the child."* (2 Kings 4:29)

Most likely the Shunammite woman heard of the miracles done by Moses and Aaron using a staff or rod:

> *And Moses said unto the people, Fear ye not, stand still, and see the salvation of the Lord, which he will shew to you today: for the Egyptians whom ye have seen today, ye shall see them again no more forever. The Lord shall fight for you, and ye shall hold your peace. And the Lord said unto Moses, wherefore criest thou unto me? speak unto the children of Israel, that they go forward: But lift thou up thy rod, and stretch out thine hand over the sea, and divide it: and the children of Israel shall go on dry ground through the midst of the sea.* (Exodus 14:13-16)

Throughout the Old Testament, the staff and rod were symbols of God's authority, given to the prophet, and God's work through him. It seems then that the most sensible thing for the Shunammite woman to do was to run back with Elisha's servant and his staff. Surely Elisha's words were comforting to her. We read in Psalm 23, *"Thy rod and Thy staff they comfort me."* But should she have run back with the servant and staff? Her decision would bring either life or continuing death to her son. From the moment her son took his last breath, she knew she had to find Elisha, the most anointed man on earth. God had granted him a double portion of Elijah's spirit. With a made-up mind, she let everyone know that she would only accept Elisha himself. She did not run for miles to replace the prophet with his servant and his staff. Believing in Elisha and her God, she knows that nothing can replace them.

> In both the Old and New Testaments, the word... 'test' means 'to prove by trial.' Therefore, when God tests His children, His purpose is to prove that our faith is real. Not that God needs to prove it to Himself since He knows all things, but He is proving to us that our faith is real, that we are truly His children, and that no trial will overcome our faith. The testing or trials we undergo come in various ways. Becoming a Christian will often require us to move out of our comfort zones and into the unknown. Perseverance in testing results in spiritual maturity and completeness. This is why James wrote, "Consider it pure joy, my brothers, whenever you face trials of many kinds" *(Got Questions)*.

TAKE HIS STAFF OR TRUST GOD.

"And the mother of the child said, As the Lord liveth, and as thy soul liveth, I will not leave thee. And he arose and followed her. And Gehazi passed on before them and laid the staff upon the face of the child." (2 Kings 4:30-31)

When you find yourself in trials that test your faith, do you believe the words of someone else over God's promises? Do their words become the staff in your life, replacing God? When you find yourself outside of God's will, you find it easier to accept a staff rather than wait on God and His promises. Moses told God's people, *"Fear ye not, stand still, and see the salvation of the Lord, which he will shew to you today."* In their obedience, the Israelites witnessed the fulfilment of God's salvation at the Red Sea. Just a short time later, however, the people agreed to replace their God with a false god, so Aaron made for them a golden calf to worship.

While Moses met with God on Mount Sinai, the people grew impatient waiting. They forgot their God, who had done great works in Egypt, wondrous works in the land of Ham, and awesome things by the Red Sea. Therefore, God said that He would destroy them. He would have, if not for Moses seeking God's mercy and forgiveness for them. As a result, God turned away His wrath and did not destroy them.

"But seek ye first the kingdom of God, and his righteousness; and all these things shall be added unto you." (Matthew 6:33)

The Shunammite woman's actions challenge all of us to seek God, His kingdom, and His righteousness. The question you need to ask yourself is whether you are seeking God's kingdom and His righteousness. Before you give an answer that may embarrass you when you stand before God, there is something you should know: God keeps records of our conversations, revealing our true motives and desires.

> *Then they that feared the Lord spake often one to another: and the Lord hearkened, and heard it, and a book of remembrance was written before him for them that feared the Lord, and that thought upon his name. And they shall be mine, saith the Lord of hosts, in that day when I make up my jewels; and I will spare them, as a man spareth his own son that serveth him.* (Malachi 3:16-17)

When you fear the Lord (in other words, when you respect, honor, and love Him), you will speak often to your friends about Him. What are the scribes in heaven writing on the pages in your book? When your book is open in heaven, will it reveal your love for God and His kingdom, or will your pages reveal your love for the things of the world? The Shunammite woman spoke often of her God. I believe that out of her conversations, He saw her greatness. In the same way, you are dictating your life story by your daily conversation and prayers. One way we can speak to our friends about God is through our prayer life. *"Rejoice evermore. Pray without ceasing. In everything give thanks: for this is the will of God in Christ Jesus concerning you."* (1 Thessalonians 5:16-18)

Your attitude speaks volumes to your family and friends. When you are unhappy, everyone knows by the look on your face and by your lack of involvement with friends and family. God tells us to rejoice: *"Whom, having not seen, ye love; in whom, though now ye see him not, yet believing, ye rejoice with joy unspeakable and full of glory: Receiving the end of your faith, even the salvation of your souls."* (1 Peter 1:8-9)

The Shunammite mother's faith gave her a spirit of joy that shone on her face. Everyone that asked, "How are you doing?" received the same answer: "It is well." Her joy convinced everyone; she was full of His glory and received the end of her faith. We too are to pray without ceasing. You might think she had an advantage over you because she made a place where she could meet Elisha and share her needs with him. If you believe that she created an environment that gave her an advantage, then do the same in your own prayer times.

> God may not answer all your prayers in a positive way or give you everything you ask.

God may not answer all your prayers in a positive way or give you everything you ask. A perfect example is the prayer Jesus prayed in the Garden of Gethsemane. In His prayer, He asked His Father, to let the cup of suffering pass from Him, if possible. He stated this three times, but it was not His Father's will to pass the cup. His will for His son was the cross at Calvary. I have heard some say, "Why did his Father not answer His prayer?" The truth of the matter is that Jesus' own words answered His prayer, proving He had already surrendered to His Father's plan. Jesus said, ***"Father not my will, but Yours be done"*** (Luke 22:42). In effect, Jesus was saying to the Father: "Your will I accept, and your plan I will finish." We should all be so bold, closing every prayer with, "Father not my will, but Yours be done."

If we could enter the Garden of Gethsemane today, I think our prayer would be like the one Jesus prayed: "Father, let this cup of afflictions pass from me," repeating it again and again, hoping God would say, "My child, I will." However, if God removes our cup, our faith and our need to depend on Him weaken. We can find His answer in Scripture:

> *The righteous cry, and the Lord heareth, and delivered them out of all their troubles. The Lord is nigh unto them that are of a broken heart; and saveth such as be of a contrite spirit. Many are the afflictions of the righteous: but the Lord delivereth him out of them all.*
> (Psalm 34:17-19)

When we find ourselves in trouble as the Shunammite woman did, our first reaction is to cry to the Lord. If God answers your prayer by removing your cup, you will have no need to cry out to Him when you find yourself in trouble. Slowly, you will lose the need to pray. How many times have you heard someone in trouble call out the name of JESUS? It is a natural reaction. Those of you who are spiritually lost, when you cry out, don't stop with just His name. Continue with, "Lord, I admit I am a sinner. Please forgive me. Amen."

If God answers your prayer and removes your cup of broken hearts, that would be awesome, but it would come to you at a great cost. You would never feel His closeness: *"The Lord is nigh unto them that are of a broken heart."* Remember the times the Lord drew close to you? Remember how being in His presence made you feel His love and compassion, while healing your brokenness?

If God removed your contrite spirit—the feeling of remorse affected by guilt—you would not experience His forgiveness and salvation.

> *For thus saith the high and lofty One that inhabiteth eternity, whose name is Holy; I dwell in the high and holy place, with him also that is of a contrite and humble spirit, to revive the spirit of the humble, and to revive the heart of the contrite ones.* (Isaiah 57:15)

You would not experience His power to transform your life.

If God removed your cup of afflictions, you would not know His power to deliver you:

> *And he said unto me, my grace is sufficient for thee: for my strength is made perfect in weakness. Most gladly therefore will I rather glory in my infirmities, that the power of Christ may rest upon me.* (2 Corinthians 12:9)

I guess we can say, "Thank God for His personal touch in our lives."

The Shunammite woman's confidence in Elisha derived from their many conversations over the years, resulting in their close friendship. The more time you spend in prayer with God, the more you learn of His character and what pleases Him and the more you depend on Him for your needs. This pleases God. She was totally dependent on her Lord and friend.

How do you ask the Creator of the Universe to be your friend? The truth of the matter is that He beat you to it. *"Henceforth, I call you not servants; for the servant knoweth not what his lord doeth: but I have called you friends; for all things that I have heard of my Father I have made known unto you."* (John 15:15)

Networking is not a new concept. Look at how God used networking to bring together total strangers to work His will in a woman's life, then you will understand the importance of networking in your personal life. Elijah, Elisha, Gehazi, the young man, and the Shunammite woman had no idea of God's plan or the role they would play in it. Through it all, they built unshakable friendships. It is the same with you. God networks people so they can succeed. Take the opportunity to learn how others can help you and how you can help them.

Connecting Elijah and Elisha was step one in God's plan for the miracle of the Shunammite woman's son, even before he was formed in her womb. Then Elisha asked Elijah for a double portion of Elijah's spirit when God took Elijah. The Shunammite woman was right from the very beginning. She knew that Elisha was anointed, not his staff. She understood that she had to persuade Elisha to go with her and do what only God could do through him: to raise her son from death to life. She is an example for all of us to place our faith in God alone.

> *And Gehazi passed on before them and laid the staff upon the face of the child; but there was neither voice, nor hearing. Wherefore, he went again to meet Elisha and the Shunammite woman, and said her child was not awake.* (2 Kings 4:31)

She was not surprised that the staff had no effect on her son. God was pleased by her faith and her total trust in Him. In verse 32; Elisha came to the room which the Shunammite woman had built for Him. Entering, he found her son's lifeless body. He prayed to the Lord; then he laid on the child, and his flesh became warm. Again, he went up and stretched himself upon him, and the child sneezed seven times, then opened his eyes. He called his mother to take up her child. Falling at Elisha's feet, she bowed and worshiped God. Afterward, she took her son.

After all she endured—the unexpected death of her son, the trip to Mount Carmel to find the prophet, and the return trip home to her son's lifeless body—her son was alive again. Even so, before embracing him, she took time to show her thankfulness and to reverence God and his servant. The next time God answers your prayer by healing a family member or friend, before celebrating, do as this mother. She first took time to kneel, and she embraced God in a prayer of thanksgiving, calling on Jehovah Rapha.

Here is what I notice: she did not let the miracle of her son's resurrection distract her from keeping her eyes on the Healer. Another thing I learned about this mother: she did not chase after the miracle during her ordeal. The entire time, she was chasing after God. Miracles alone do not produce faith. Your faith will produce miracles. Are you chasing miracles? If so, stop and start chasing God.

YOU ARE CALLED TO DO GREATER WORKS.

> *Verily, verily, I say unto you, He that believeth in me, the works that I do shall he do also; and **greater works than these shall he do,** because I go unto my Father. And whatsoever ye shall ask in my name, that will I do, that the Father may be glorified in the Son. If ye shall ask anything in my name, I will do it.* (John 14:12-14)

Today, the prophets no longer walk the earth carrying staffs and rods, performing miracles. God has replaced the rod and staff of the Old Testament with the gifts of the Spirit. The Holy Spirit now serves as the intermediary for believers by delivering messages and teachings from God. *"But the Comforter, which is the Holy Ghost, whom the Father will send in my name, he shall teach you all things, and bring all things to your remembrance, whatsoever I have said unto you."* (John 14:26)

Before you start thinking, doubting, and imagining that you cannot do greater works than Jesus, I tell you that you can and you will. Jesus said to all believers, "verily, verily," which means "in truth, with certainty, and confidence, you will do greater works." I understand that greater works may seem out of reach for some believers, so let's take the first step. It is time to equip yourself. There are two spiritual areas I would like to introduce to you.

The first spiritual area includes the gifts of the Holy Spirit. The apostle Paul said:

Now concerning spiritual gifts, brethren, I do not want you to be ignorant, for to one is given the word of wisdom through the Spirit, to another the word of knowledge through the same Spirit, to another faith by the same Spirit, to another gifts of healings by the same Spirit, to another the working of miracles, to another prophecy, to another discerning of spirits, to another different kinds of tongues, to another the interpretation of tongues. But one and the same Spirit works all these things, distributing to each one individually as He wills. (1 Corinthians 12:1; 8-11)

I believe that the gifts of the Spirit are for today's church.

During my twenty-four years serving as Chaplain at Escambia County Florida Corrections, I've had the privilege to work with several Protestant groups. On the topic of the gifts of the Spirit there are different opinions among our groups. Some believe the gifts ceased with the death of the apostles, some believe that not all gifts are meant for today's church, and others believe that all the gifts are active in the Body of Christ. I believe that the gifts of the Spirit are for today's church. Consider this: Jesus calls you to do greater works. Without the use of the spiritual gifts of wisdom, knowledge, faith, healing, miracles, prophecy, discerning of spirits, tongues, and interpretation, we may feel powerless, but take heart! God gives these gifts abundantly.

YOUNG GIRL, REALIZE THE TRUTH OF HIS GIFTS.

One Sunday morning after services, one of our young girls asked me to pray for her. Kneeling, I asked her what she needed. She said, "I have a test next week." "Well," I said, "let's ask God to give you the knowledge needed and bring to your remembrance the material you studied while you were preparing for the test." To my surprise and joy, she said, "Pastor wouldn't that be cheating?" With a big smile, I said, "No, honey. Wisdom and knowledge are God's gift to you and to all who believe in Him."

THE PROPHET'S STAFF: A SYMBOL OF GOD'S PROTECTION

Finally, my brethren, be strong in the Lord, and in the power of his might. Put on the whole armor of God, that ye may be able to stand against the wiles of the devil. For we wrestle not against flesh and blood, but against principalities, against powers, against the rulers of the darkness of this world, against spiritual wickedness in high places. Wherefore take unto you the whole armor of God, that ye may be able to withstand in the evil day, and having done all, to stand. Stand therefore, having your loins girt about with truth, and having on the breastplate of righteousness. (Ephesians 6:10-14)

Today the prophet's staff, also known as a shepherd's staff, has been replaced with the armor of God. The Shunammite woman never heard the term "armor of God," but we can see by her actions that she demonstrated His armor. Throughout her life, she stayed strong in the Lord as she walked with Him, learning the power of His might. Not by her might, but by God's was she able to stand against the tricks of Satan and death. *"Then he answered and spake unto me, saying, this is the word of the Lord unto Zerubbabel, saying, Not by might, nor by power, but by my spirit, saith the Lord of hosts."* (Zechariah 4:6) Somehow, she understood that her fight was not against flesh and blood. She was fighting forces that she could not see, so she gave the fight to the Lord. Follow her lead and give the fight to the Lord. Let God unveil your unseen enemy.

Wherefore take unto you the whole armor of God, that ye may be able to withstand in the evil day, and having done all, to stand. Stand therefore, having your loins girt about with truth, and having on the breastplate of righteousness; And your feet shod with the preparation of the gospel of peace; Above all, taking the shield of faith, wherewith ye shall be able to quench all the fiery darts of the wicked. And take the helmet of salvation, and the sword of the Spirit, which is the word of God. (Ephesians 6:13-17)

Are you ready to do greater works? Then get familiar with your armor.

Although prophets still play a major role in God's church today, He is calling for all believers to trust and believe on His promises as this woman did. Together we can do greater works. Let's lay down the staffs and rods of old and use the gifts of the Spirit. Put on His armor.

"Praying always with all prayer and supplication in the Spirit and watching thereunto with all perseverance and supplication for all saints." (Ephesians 6:18)

SO LAY DOWN THE STAFFS AND RODS AND TAKE UP THE GIFTS OF HIS SPIRIT.

NOTES:

10: EVIDENCE

*"Now faith is the substance of things hoped for and the **evidence** of things not seen."* (Hebrews 11:1)

EVIDENCE

Suggests serving as proof of the actuality or existence of something.

Throughout the Scriptures, the Shunammite woman was confident, never doubting her God was real. Have you ever had someone question your Christian faith and beliefs, asking you to show them the evidence that your God really exists? God has given each of us a charge, as Christians, to explain our beliefs: *"But sanctify the Lord God in your hearts: and be ready always to give an answer to every man that asketh you, a reason of the hope that is in you, with meekness and fear."* (1 Peter 3:15)

As I mentioned earlier in my book, I serve as Chaplain at Escambia County Correction in Pensacola Florida. While in phase II, on the second floor in green pod, I was handing out Bibles and praying with the inmates. Suddenly, one of them said, "If you really believe in your God, then prove to us that He exists." Well, I didn't expect to be put on the spot in the presence of twenty other inmates who were listening in the dorm, but I gladly accepted the challenge. I told everyone that I would go to my office and bring back the proof.

Back at my desk with my Bible and commentary, I wrote notes and searched the Scripture that explained the creation of everything we see and know, including the story of the birth of God's son. Then I heard God ask me, "What are you doing?" I answered, "I am proving your existence to the inmates." He said, "You can't. Just be a witness; I will do the rest." I still thought that there must be something I could do or say that would convince them of God's existence, but He reminded me of His conversation with Peter and the disciples.

Soon, I returned to the pod that housed the twenty inmates with only five verses. The inmates gathered around to hear what I had to say, and the inmate who challenged me said, "Show me the proof." I told him that I would first read the Scripture to everyone.

> *When Jesus came into the coasts of Caesarea Philippi, he asked his disciples, saying, whom do men say that I the Son of man am? And they said, some say that thou art John the Baptist: some, Elias; and others, Jeremias, or one of the prophets. He saith unto them, but who say ye that I am? And Simon Peter answered and said, Thou art the Christ, the Son of the living God. And Jesus answered and said unto him, Blessed art thou, Simon Barjona: for flesh and blood hath not revealed it unto thee, but my Father which is in heaven.* (Matthew 16:13-17)

Then turning to the inmate, I said, "I set out to prove to you and these men that my God does exist, but after reading these verses, God convinced me that what I am doing is a futile act, because only God can reveal Himself to you. I can't. If the scripture is the proof of God's existence, then everyone who reads the Bible would be believers, but we know this is not the case. When God reveals Himself to you through the Scriptures, then you will never doubt His authenticity."

God has revealed Himself many times in the Bible, each time unveiling more of His character. In the Garden of Eden, He revealed Himself as the One who created us in His image and likeness and the Father who seeks His children when we go astray. To Abraham, He revealed Himself as the One who longs to have a friendship with us. To Jonah, He revealed Himself as the One who condemns sin, but not the person, for He loves the sinners and forgives their sins. *"If we confess our sins, he is faithful and just to forgive us our sins, and to cleanse us from all unrighteousness."* (1 John

1:9) Then on the cross, He sacrificed Himself so that you and I might have eternal life.

God revealed Himself to the Shunammite woman through His prophet Elisha. The evidence is seen in her speech, her attitude, and her actions. She spoke with confidence, things that were not, as though they were. In faith, she believed. Of course, it is not about the power of her words nor ours; it is about the power of God's promises and His faithfulness to keep them.

Could it be that God has revealed Himself to you, but you have rejected the spirit of truth? Many were present on the day that Jesus was baptized. God used this sacred event to unveil the Holy Trinity. Things that were unseen, He displayed to the world, showing evidence of each one individually. God told everyone that Jesus is His beloved Son in whom He is well pleased.

> *And Jesus, when he was baptized, went up straightway out of the water: and, lo, the heavens were opened unto him, and he saw the Spirit of God descending like a dove, and lighting upon him. And lo a voice from heaven, saying, this is my beloved Son, in whom I am well pleased.* (Matthew 3:16-17)

On that day, God separated Himself from all the false gods, claiming the title that is rightfully His: the one and only true, living God. *"And this is life eternal, that they might know thee, the only true God, and Jesus Christ, whom thou hast sent."* (John 17:3) The fact that the heavens opened unto Jesus is very important because it supports the Scripture and the Lord's prayer: "Our Father who art in heaven, hallowed be Thy name." God's speaking to the people and to His son from heaven is proof that He is the Father of Jesus and our God. Everyone heard Him validate His son, telling the world He is pleased with Him.

"Hallowed be your name." (Matthew 6:9) "Hallowed" in the original Greek is "hagiazo," and it means "to make, render, or declare as sacred or holy, or to mentally venerate or revere." Those who came to the baptism

heard and saw the evidence. Many believed, but not everyone. My prayer for you if you're not a born-again believer is for God to reveal Himself to you and for you to believe and repent. *"Jesus answered and said unto him, 'Verily, verily, I say unto thee, except a man be born again, he cannot see the kingdom of God.'"* (John 3:3)

GOD OPENS ELISHA'S SERVANT'S EYES.

> *And when the servant of the man of God was risen early, and gone forth, behold, an host compassed the city both with horses and chariots. And his servant said unto him, Alas, my master! How shall we do? And he answered, Fear not: for they that be with us are more than they that be with them.* (2 Kings 6:15-16)

We know that we are to walk by faith and not by sight, but there are times in our life that sight will increase our faith. Here, God uses both to conquer the servant's fears. I don't care how much faith you may have, there will come a time when you need to see the proof that He is moving in your circumstances.

Elisha knew his servant needed more than just being told that "they that be with us are more than they that be with them." The servant's eyes had already convinced him that they could not win the fight. Has your sight convinced you the challenges in life are more that you can endure? Do you feel alone, thinking you cannot win? Elisha asked God to open his servant's eyes so that he could see the unseen army standing on the mountain ready to fight for them.

"And Elisha prayed, and said, Lord, I pray thee open his eyes, that he may see. And the Lord opened the eyes of the young man; and he saw: and behold, the mountain was full of horses and chariots of fire round about Elisha." (2 Kings 6:17)

This is my prayer for you: that God will open your eyes, that you can see every promise that God has designed especially for you, each standing tall and strong as chariots of fire with His angels ready to perform His promises. Concerning your needs, just put your trust in God, for He has you in his hands. Amen. *"But my God shall supply all your need according to his riches in glory by Christ Jesus."* (Philippians 4:19)

LIFE IN THE WORDS OF A STRANGER (JOHN 4).

In John 4, Jesus came to the city of Sychar in Samaria to a parcel of land that Jacob had given to his sons where he dug a well, known as Jacob's well. Being the 6th hour, Jesus stopped to rest. In Jewish time, noon was the 6th hour of the day. He sent His disciples into the city to buy some meat. A woman came from the city to draw water. Seeing a Jewish man sitting on the well made her nervous because the Jews had no dealings with her kind.

To her surprise, Jesus asked her for a drink of water. She replied, "I can't believe you, being a Jew, would ask me to give you a drink of water, my being a woman of Samaria." Then he said to her, "If you knew who asked you for a drink of water, you would ask me for a drink of living water."

In the last day, that great day of the feast, Jesus stood and cried, saying, if any man thirst, let him come unto me, and drink. He that believeth on me, as the scripture hath said, out of his belly shall flow rivers of living water. (John 7:37-38)

She noticed He had no rope or bucket to draw from the well. Knowing the well was deep, she asked Him, "Where is this living water you told me about?" He responded, "Those who drink water from Jacob's well will never be satisfied and will thirst again, but this water I want to give you, you will never thirst again, for this water shall become a well of water springing up inside of you into everlasting life." Then she said, "Sir, give me this water that I may drink and thirst not."

The woman at the well still saw Jesus as a "Jewish guy," but this would soon change because He was about to get very personal with His questions. He asked her to go get her husband, to which she responded that she had no husband. Jesus said, "You tell the truth. You have had five husbands, and the man you are now living with is not your husband." Let's take a moment to learn what just happened and how it applies to our own lives. Jesus may have planned the meeting at the well, but what amazes me is that He kept His identity a secret. Using only His words, He convinced her that He was more than a prophet. So, when witnessing, just be yourself. Let the Holy Spirit speak through you, then His words will be the evidence of God's existence as He reveals himself through your conversation.

Here's a short testimony where I concealed my identity. The Escambia County Sheriff's Department has a golf league; they play one Saturday a month. Al, a friend of mine and a captain on the force, asked me to join their league. I told him I would join on one condition—that he not tell the officers I am a chaplain. When the moment was right, I would tell them. He agreed. Standing on the first tee, I met my team members. After greeting one another, off we went, and so did their language, and the jokes.

> "I wanted to know the real you, not the fake you."

After finishing the front nine, while standing on the tenth tee box, I asked what they did on the force. They told me, and one of them asked what department I worked in. "I'm the chaplain," I said. Immediately, each man apologized for his language and jokes, asking why I didn't tell them I was a chaplain. I said, "I wanted to know the real you, not the fake you." Jesus sat with sinners, and He was an example for all of us. By the time the third outing came around, all the officers had heard that I was the chaplain. I made many friends on the force. The next time a friend asks you to join him for golfing, fishing, or to a ball game, don't wear your "All Sinners Go to Hell" t-shirt. Instead, take the opportunity to have fun, learn from their conversation the things they like to do, use what you learn to be a friend, and let them see Christ in you, not on your shirt.

The woman at the well is an awesome story, but there is much more to her story than her five failed marriages and the fact that the man she lived with was not her husband. I am sure you have heard many messages on this topic, and some are not so nice concerning her lifestyle. God helps us to always see the good in people, so the first thing I notice is how Jesus addressed the racism that separated the Jewish people from the Samaritans. Presenting Himself as a Jewish man was His first step in removing her belief that she was unworthy to be in His company. Think about this: if you were at the well, would you cause a sinner to feel awkward in your presence because they knew you were a Christian and Christians have no dealings with sinners? Would your conversation be the evidence of God and his love for them, or would your words be condemning?

Again, Jesus' conversation changed. It was no longer about her personal life, but about how and where to worship God. She said, "Our fathers worshipped on this mountain, but you say Jerusalem is the place to worship." He said to her that the hour had come when how you worship the Father is what is important. To be a true worshipper, you must worship Him in Spirit and truth, for the Father seeks such to worship Him.

You're not going to have a spiritual awakening just by being on a mountain top, nor in Jerusalem. There is a new way to worship the Father, and that is in Spirit and in truth. Again, Jesus showed more of his real identity as He continued to speak to the Samaritan woman. She said, "I remember being told the Messiah would come, which is the Christ, and He would tell us all things, like you have told me the things about myself." Jesus, the Jewish man, would now unveil His real identity. He said to her, "You have been talking to the Christ all this time, for I am He."

As Jesus' disciples returned, they marveled that Jesus was talking with the Samaritan woman. In her excitement and believing He was the Christ, she left her waterpot behind and went to tell the others in the city. She said to the people in the city, "Come see a man that told me all things I ever did. Is this not the Christ?" When I read "come see a man that told me **all things I ever did,**" I realize she and Jesus had an in-depth conversation about her life. If Jesus had only mentioned the bad things in her life—meaning the five husbands and the guy she was living with—this would not have gotten her excited because that was common knowledge in her city. I am convinced that their conversation was like the one that God had with the churches in Revelations.

When speaking to the churches in chapters 2 and 3 of Revelations, Jesus started each conversation by telling them all the good things He saw in them. Then He said, "Nevertheless, I have something against thee." Likewise, I believe Jesus told her all the good things He saw in her and told her the secret things both good and bad that only she knew about herself. He convinced her He was more than a prophet. Then as with the churches, he said, "Nevertheless, I have something against you," and told her the things she needed to work on. This is why she told the people in the city to come see a man who told her **everything she ever did**. We, too, have this conversation with God. After telling us all the good we have done, He says, "Nevertheless, I have some things against you."

Your friends and neighbors will see God in you when you start looking beyond the bad you may have heard or seen in a person and find the good in them. So, start by being a real Christian. Be Christlike. Jesus sat with sinners, so begin with your neighbor next door—the one that for years, your only contact was a hand-wave. Invite them to your next cookout. Chances are you will make a friend as you share with them a drink of the living water Jesus gave to you.

The people in Samaria learned that Jesus came for whomever would call upon Him:

> *There is neither Jew nor Greek, there is neither bond nor free, there is neither male nor female: for ye are all one in Christ Jesus. And if ye be Christ's, then are ye Abraham's seed, and heirs according to the promise.* (Galatians 3:28-29)

FAITH: "Having complete confidence or trust in a person or thing." You will find confidence in others when you start believing in yourself, knowing that you too can do what is right. Likewise, you will start trusting in others when you begin trusting in yourself through Christ.

SUBSTANCE: "The subject matter of thought." What are you thinking? What is on your mind? What subject consumes you this week? Knowing each of our thoughts, God penned this verse: *"Casting down imaginations, and every high thing that exalteth itself against the knowledge of God and **bringing into captivity every thought to the obedience of Christ."** (2 Corinthians 10:5)

HOPE: "The feeling that what is wanted can be had or that events will turn out for the best."

The Shunammite woman felt that what she wanted could be had, but it was her faith in God that moved Him to give her the desire of her heart. As she prayed, you must also pray for the things you want. By faith, believe it can be had and that it will turn out for the best.

The Shunammite woman is evidence of what happens when, by faith, we totally trust in God. Her faith convinces her husband to build a room for Elisha on the side of their home. Then, although she first rejects God's promise of a son, God uses her faith to convert her negative thoughts into obedience toward the hope of His promise. Her

faith proves that things unseen will manifest: God raises her son from death to life! There is no doubt as to why God calls her great. Her great faith causes her to be a great woman.

EVIDENCE: Proof of the actuality or existence of something.

SO, IT'S UP TO YOU—BE THE EVIDENCE.

NOTES:

ABOUT THE AUTHOR

Willie Tracy Leggett—affectionately known as Pastor Tracy—has dedicated nearly three decades to serving as a chaplain, pastor, and mentor to inmates, correctional officers, and their families at the Escambia County Correctional Facility in Pensacola, Florida. A passionate and faithful minister of the Gospel, he also leads New Vision Worship Center in Milton, Florida, where he continues to shepherd his congregation with unwavering love and truth.

An ordained minister with the International Pentecostal Holiness Church, Pastor Tracy serves within the ALPHA Conference and is committed to preaching the transformative message of Jesus Christ. With a heart full of faith and a spirit of encouragement, he speaks life, hope, and the promises of God wherever he goes.

For more than 43 years, Pastor Tracy and his wife, Radena, have walked hand in hand in life and in faith—ministering together for 39 of those years with hearts devoted to God's service. Together, they have raised four children, delight in their eight grandchildren, and have become spiritual parents to many.

Through his writing, Pastor Tracy seeks to draw readers into a deeper awareness of God's presence, strengthen their relationship with the Creator, and proclaim the faithfulness of God to fulfill every promise.

To God be the glory!

www.ingramcontent.com/pod-product-compliance
Lightning Source LLC
LaVergne TN
LVHW051249080426
835513LV00016B/1823